Cooking Well

The New
Kitchen
Garden

Hatherleigh Press is committed to preserving and protecting the natural resources of the Earth. Environmentally responsible and sustainable practices are embraced within the company's mission statement.

Hatherleigh Press is a member of the Publishers Earth Alliance, committed to preserving and protecting the natural resources of the planet while developing a sustainable business model for the book publishing industry.

This book was edited and designed in the village of Hobart, New York. Hobart is a community that has embraced books and publishing as a component of its livelihood. There are several unique bookstores in the village. For more information, please visit www.hobartbookvillage.com.

www.hatherleighpress.com

DISCLAIMER
This book offers general cooking and eating suggestions for educational purposes only. In no case should it be a substitute nor replace a healthcare professional. Consult your healthcare professional to determine which foods are safe for you and to establish the right diet for your personal nutritional needs.

Library of Congress Cataloging-in-Publication Data

The new kitchen garden.
    p. cm. -- (Cooking well)
  Includes bibliographical references.
  ISBN 978-1-57826-331-8 (pbk. : alk. paper) 1. Cooking. 2. Cooking (Natural foods) I. Hatherleigh Press.
  TX714.N494 2010
  641.5'636--dc22

                            2010024954

All Hatherleigh Press titles are available for bulk purchase, special promotions, and premiums. For information about reselling and special purchase opportunities, please call 1-800-528-2550 and ask for the Special Sales Manager.

Cover Design by Nick Macagnone
Cover Photography by Catarina Astrom
Interior Design by Nick Macagnone

10 9 8 7 6 5 4 3 2 1

hatherleigh
Improve your life. Change your world.

Acknowledgments

We would like to extend a special thank you to Jo Brielyn and Christina Anger—without your hard work and creativity this book would not have been possible.

Table of Contents

Chapter 1

Kitchen Garden
Basics

In recent years, the time-honored tradition of home gardening has made a comeback and continues to gain interest. Most people today are searching for time-saving and frugal methods of growing, maintaining, and harvesting plants in their own gardens. They are also more concerned with the quality of their crops, rather than quantity alone. Due to these needs and the ever-growing focus on cooking with and eating organic foods, the kitchen garden is a concept many individuals and families are embracing.

What is a Kitchen Garden?

For those unfamiliar with it, the term "kitchen garden" may invoke images of small potted plants and herbs on the kitchen windowsill. However, the majority of kitchen gardens are actually located outside of the house, although it is certainly possible to grow a few choice culinary plants indoors. By definition, a kitchen garden is an outdoor garden, located in close proximity to the cooking area of a home, in which items to be used in the kitchen are grown. The plants in a typical kitchen garden are intended to provide for the members of a household, not to be resold or distributed. They are to be eaten immediately, prepared in a meal the same day they are picked, or preserved to use later when the item is out of season.

Unlike a traditional vegetable garden, a kitchen garden serves a dual purpose: to supply fresh herbs and produce for the household and to function as a part of the home's landscape. It is sited near the house, often among the decorative plants and flowers in the main lawn, not tucked away in a remote location. While vegetables are often considered the main residents in the kitchen garden, other plants like herbs, fruits, and edible flowers may also be added. Plants chosen for inclusion in the garden are selected for their aesthetically pleasing features as well as their culinary functions. In essence, a kitchen garden is edible landscaping.

Staple crops that make appearances in most kitchen gardens are tomatoes, lettuces and salad greens, peppers, cucumbers, squashes, and melons. Popular culinary herbs such as basil, thyme, oregano, dill, and parsley are also commonly grown. Some edible flowers used in kitchen gardens, such as lavender, add beauty to the plot and have beneficial medicinal or culinary qualities when harvested. Others, such as marigolds and nasturtiums, are planted to function as pest deterrents throughout the garden. Ultimately, however, the types of crops and plants found in a kitchen garden depend upon the individual gardener's personal preferences, needs, and space availability.

In much the same way, there are no set rules on the size or design of a kitchen garden. They may range from a small bed of just salad greens and lettuces to several raised beds that produce enough fruits, vegetable and herbs to feed a large family. Although kitchen gardens are customarily geometric in design, one can be plotted in virtually any shape to meet specific requirements or to fit the space a gardener has available.

Individuals who live in urban areas or have little lawn to work with need not sacrfice fresh, home-grown produce. Kitchen gardens are quite flexible, and with the help of a little ingenuity, most areas are able to accommodate at least a small garden. There are also other options available for growing or acquiring fresh fruits and vegetables, which will be addressed in the next chapter.

The Benefits of a Kitchen Garden

You may wonder why, with the large variety of produce and herbs readily accessible in grocery stores and markets, it is beneficial for you to have your own kitchen garden. The benefits of a kitchen garden are numerous. The three most significant are: cost, taste and quality, and health.

Growing vegetables, fruits and herbs in your kitchen garden will save you money. Even when you include the costs of setting up and maintaining the garden, you will be spending far less for your fresh produce and herbs by growing them yourself as opposed to buying them in a supermarket. Purchasing a package of tomatoes for a few dollars in a grocery store may not seem like much, but when you consider how many tomatoes can be grown from one plant purchased for the same price, the savings are significant. You also save on gas because a trip to the grocery store is no longer necessary. Instead, you simply step into your own yard to pick what you need.

Home grown items are fresher and taste better. Produce and herbs available in the store are often older than they appear. They are picked before fully ripe, sprayed to prevent them from ripening as quickly, and then stored until bought. The end result is tough, chewy, and less flavorful foods. When you pluck items from your own kitchen garden, you can select only young produce that is ripe and fresh, and you can harvest as it is needed. Fruits are juicier, vegetables are crisper, and herbs are fresher. You will find all of them to be more flavorful.

Food grown in your kitchen garden is healthier for you and your family. Commercial gardeners who provide fruits and vegetables to stores and local markets often use poisonous pesticides and other chemicals on their products. With a kitchen garden, you control what touches your food. Finding natural alternative methods for dealing with pests and bugs in your garden provides produce and herbs that are healthier for you and your family. You also get the maximum nutrients and health benefits from fruits and vegetables when you eat them as soon as they are picked. Equally important is the fresh air and exercise that you and your family will receive from working in your kitchen garden.

History of Kitchen Gardens

Although the idea of growing kitchen gardens is becoming increasingly popular in recent years, it is certainly not a new one. In fact, kitchen gardens have existed for centuries. The pleasure gardens of ancient Middle East, though much more elaborate than the typical kitchen garden, were the first gardens to incorporate fruits and vegetables into the surrounding landscape.

The first true kitchen gardens emerged years later during the Middle Ages as herb gardens were kept at monasteries. In the 18th and 19th centuries, kitchen gardens were then taken to a whole new level by French gardeners. They transformed them into beautiful works of art as well as functional gardening spaces. These potagers (the French term for kitchen gardens) introduced geometric design to kitchen garden landscaping, an attribute still evident in many today.

Colonial American families also planted kitchen gardens, staying with the basic structure but making them less formal and more practical. The victory gardens of the World War I and II eras, which were also referred to as "freedom gardens" or "war gardens", once again returned focus to kitchen gardens. People planted victory gardens to do their part to provide sustenance during wartime and to draw together as communities. Many of the victory gardens of that time were planted and maintained on communal land, where several families worked on them together. Modern kitchen gardens are a conglomeration of all these historical gardens and more.

The White House Kitchen Garden

Variations of kitchen gardens have also made their way onto the grounds of the White House. Over the years, several United States presidents and their families have broken ground to grow their own vegetables, fruits, and herbs.

- The first president to live in the White House, President John Adams, was an avid gardener and planted fruit trees, vegetables, and herbs there to help feed his family.

- During World War I, President Woodrow Wilson planted crops and even raised a flock of sheep on the White House lawn.

- In 1943, the most famous kitchen garden was established on the presidential grounds: the White House Victory Garden planted by Eleanor Roosevelt.

- While residing at 1600 Pennsylvania Avenue, President Bill Clinton and his family did not break ground to raise their own crops, but instead grew some of their favorite vegetables in pots on the White House roof.

- In 2009, President Barack Obama and his family dug up a patch of the South Lawn and planted the first vegetable garden on the grounds since the Roosevelt family occupied the premises, over sixty years ago.

Chapter 2

Tips for Starting a
Kitchen Garden

Planning Your Kitchen Garden

The first necessary step in planning your kitchen garden is assessing the space you have available for the plot. Making wise and informed decisions about the location of your garden will help ensure your success. Consider these factors when determining where to break ground for your kitchen garden:

Plants generally found in a kitchen garden require direct sunlight to thrive. For optimal growth, the plot should receive at least six hours of full sun each day. Large trees or buildings cast large shadows, so place your garden far enough that they will not be overshadowed and lose direct sunlight.

A healthy kitchen garden requires ground with good drainage. Avoid locations that are lower than the rest of the yard. Water collects there, causing the ground to remain too wet. Plants in such an environment are more susceptible to rot and generally do not yield as much product. A short walk around your yard after a rainstorm should help determine which areas tend to hold water. Stay away from these areas when plotting your kitchen garden, and instead choose a location on higher ground.

Too much shelter can be harmful to your garden. Although light cover helps protect your kitchen garden from the elements, too much shelter may promote a buildup of diseases or pests. Trees located too close to the garden will also hamper development of the plants and crops because they deprive the garden of vital moisture and nutrients.

Position your kitchen garden in a convenient and accessible location. A garden sited near the house becomes a part of the landscaping and usually receives more attention and use. The closer to your kitchen, the more you will use the garden in your daily meals. Also, most homes have a handy outside water source, and your plants will need plenty of water. Keeping the garden fairly close to your house also discourages wild animals from feasting on your plants.

The size and design of your kitchen garden are other decisions you need to make during the planning stage. Take into account the amount of space you have available in your chosen location, the appearance you hope to achieve, how many people you intend to provide for with the harvested crops, and the size requirements of the plants you wish to grow in the garden. A functional kitchen garden can be nearly any shape or size, so it is simply a matter of fitting your personal needs and preferences.

If you are planning a kitchen garden for the first time, it is recommended to start with a small, more manageable plot. Even one 4' x 4' bed, when carefully planned and cared for, will yield a good harvest and allow time for beginners to learn and enjoy maintaining the garden. A family that desires to produce enough crops to feed the entire household and also preserve some for later use may choose to make a larger kitchen garden. To avoid getting overwhelmed or taking on more work than you can handle, it is wise to begin with a smaller garden (no bigger than 10' x 20') and add to it the following year if you decide you need more.

Your kitchen garden can be built and organized in several ways. The most common methods include a traditional row garden, bed garden, square foot garden and patio garden. Again, the setup you choose for your garden will depend greatly on your space, needs, and preferences.

A traditional row garden is planted much the same way as a larger home or farm garden. It is laid out in straight, single-crop rows with access paths between each row. This method is an effective way to plant crops if you have a tiller or tractor to prepare the plot, and if you have a large space to use. The traditional row method is not used as often as the others because of these requirements. Many families planting kitchen gardens do not have access to the equipment needed to prepare the soil and need a more space-efficient approach to gardening.

A bed garden is arranged with one or several small beds located close together. Plants are placed in groups instead of rows. Bed gardens are one of the most commonly used methods for kitchen gardens because they require less space. Very little usable space is used for walkways between the beds. Many kitchen gardeners who use bed gardens choose to create raised beds. Raised beds are positioned at a more comfortable working height, and allow for better control of soil quality, drainage, and weed and pest control.

A square foot garden is a more deliberate variation of bed gardening. It makes optimal use of limited gardening space by sectioning each bed into small squares. For example, a 4' x 4' bed can be broken down into 16 small squares. Each one of those squares measures 12" x 12" and is used to host a different crop. Depending on the size and space requirements of each individual plant, one 4' x 4' box can potentially hold up to 100 plants. Planting in this type of garden is done more deliberately,

Kitchen Gardens for Urban Dwellers

Living in an urban area does not necessarily mean doing without a kitchen garden. It simply requires creativity and smart use of the space you have.

- If you have a sunny stoop or balcony, the suggestions below for patio gardening may work for you.
- Window farming is a fun, creative way to grow a few fresh vegetables. This method turns recycled plastic bottles, clay pellets, plastic tubing, and fish tank air pumps into a small indoor kitchen garden. Visit www.windowfarms. org to read more about it.
- Both indoor and outdoor window boxes can be attached to grow small plants. Keep in mind that boxes located inside will require extra lighting because they do not receive direct sunlight.

and wastes very few seeds or seedlings. Because it is a raised bed method, a square foot garden can be placed in any suitable location large enough to hold it, including decks or patios.

A patio garden is an ideal gardening solution for apartment dwellers or anyone with limited lawn space. Individuals who have a small balcony, stoop or deck with direct sunlight can make the most of the space by utilizing small raised beds, as in the square foot garden. Another option is using containers and pots to raise a small patio garden. The containers can be moved around

Basic Gardening Tools Needed for Your Kitchen Garden

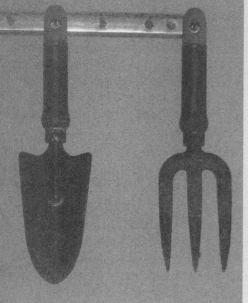

Unlike traditional gardens, only a small number of gardening tools are required for maintaining your kitchen garden. Since most kitchen gardens are kept in raised beds, maintenance is much simpler. The initial digging and planting of your garden will require the use of larger tools such as a shovel and garden rake, but after that you will generally need only a few main tools.

- **Pruners:** A quality pair of small shears for trimming plants and removing dead or diseased portions.

- **Spade:** For digging or loosening soil in the kitchen garden beds.

- **Oriental garden tool or small multi-functional tool:** For weeding, digging holes for planting seedlings or bulbs, and other small gardening tasks.

- **Hose or watering can:** To provide the necessary water to nourish plants or wash away small bugs.

to capitalize on the sunlight and they generally attract fewer soil pests. There are a variety of fruits and vegetables that grow happily in containers such as tomatoes, peppers, and spinach. Most herbs can be successfully grown in patio gardens as well.

Selecting the vegetables, fruits, herbs and edible flowers to include in your kitchen garden is an exciting part of the planning process. It is also an important one. Here are some helpful tips to remember:

Make sure plants are suitable for the hardiness zone in which you live. Not all plants will thrive in the same temperatures and conditions. Zone information is listed on most seed packages. If you plan to transplant items, research the hardiness of the plant before you purchase. However, most local greenhouses will only sell items conducive with the zone they are in.

Select varieties that grow best in your region. There are many varieties within each family of vegetables and fruits, and some are more adapted to a specific area. Plant those that are known to grow better in your region and you will see a greater harvest.

Plan for the amount of space each plant needs and plant only as much as you require. To make the best use of your garden space, do the research to determine how much room each plant will require. Also, learning the typical size of harvest you can expect from each plant will help you decide how many of them you need to include.

Grow what your family likes most. Choosing items that grow well in the area or yield a great harvest may make your garden look plentiful and healthy, but if they will not be eaten, growing them is unnecessary and wasteful. Instead, stick with produce you know will be used.

Below is a suggested list of five highly nutritious items to include in your kitchen garden and the benefits they offer to you and your family:

Tomato	Contains Lycopene, an antioxidant known to fight cancer, heart disease, high cholesterol, and other medical conditions and illnesses. Tomatoes are also rich in fiber, potassium, and vitamins A, C, and K.
Broccoli	Broccoli is packed with nutrients like vitamins A (mostly beta-carotene) and C, folic acid, calcium and fiber. It's also been linked to reducing the risk of several conditions including cataracts, high blood pressure, heart disease, arthritis, common cold viruses, and some cancers.
Strawberry	This fruit is high in disease-fighting phytonutrients and antioxidants. Strawberries also have significant levels of nutrients like vitamins C, B5, B6, and K, folic acid, potassium, magnesium, fiber, and omega-3 fatty acids.
Kale	Has a high nutrient-rich phytochemical content for fighting illnesses and provides vitamins A, B, C and K, potassium, lutein, calcium, fiber, and iron. Kale also contains enzymes that detoxify cancer-causing chemicals.
Endive	A leafy green vegetable that aids in gastric and digestive problems. Endive contains essential B1, B2, C, K and P vitamins, amino acids, potassium, calcium, iron, and magnesium.

Preparing and Planting Your Kitchen Garden

Once you have determined what items you will grow in your garden, it is time to prepare for planting. Knowing when to plant in your garden is key to the success of its growth and should be determined early on. Plants placed in the ground too early may not survive and those rooted too late may never reach full maturity. Planting should not happen until after the average last spring frost date for your area.

After the proper planting time has been established, follow the directions on each seed packet for sowing seeds indoors if you intend to transplant later. Seeds generally need to be started about 6 to 8 weeks before the last frost date.

Frost Chart by Zones	
Zone 1	Average dates of last frost - June, 1 to June, 30 Average dates of first frost - July, 1 to July, 31
Zone 2	Average dates of last frost - May, 1 to May, 31 Average dates of first frost - August, 1 to August, 31
Zone 3	Average dates of last frost - May, 1 to May, 31 Average dates of first frost - September, 1 to September, 30
Zone 4	Average dates of last frost - May, 1 to May, 30 Average dates of first frost - September, 1 to September, 30
Zone 5	Average dates of last frost - March, 30 to April, 30 Average dates of first frost - September, 30 to October, 30
Zone 6	Average dates of last frost - March, 30 to April, 30 Average dates of first frost - September, 30 to October, 30
Zone 7	Average dates of last frost - March, 30 to April, 30 Average dates of first frost - September, 30 to October, 30
Zone 8	Average dates of last frost - February, 28 to March, 30 Average dates of first frost - October, 30 to November, 30
Zone 9	Average dates of last frost - January, 30 to February, 28 Average dates of first frost - November, 30 to December, 30
Zone 10	Average dates of last frost - January, 30 or before Average dates of first frost - November, 30 to December, 30
Zone 11	Free of Frost throughout the year

(Chart provided by Avant-Gardening: Creative Organic Gardening: www.avant-gardening.com/zone.htm)

You may also decide to purchase small plants from a local greenhouse and transplant them into your kitchen garden. Keep these things in mind when selecting your items:

Check the leaves of all plants. Avoid any that have pale or mottled leaves. Be sure to also look on the underside of the leaves for signs of insects or disease.

Avoid plants that are wilted. Look for healthier ones.

Do not buy plants that have roots growing out of the bottom of the pot or pack. Transplanting them will break off some of their roots.

Do not select plants that are already flowering or fruiting. They are too mature.

No lawn contains perfect soil for gardening, so it is beneficial to prepare the garden soil before planting time. Basic soil tests can be conducted to determine the type of soil you have, as well as the acidity and alkalinity of your soil. Do-it-yourself kits can be purchased and many local services offer free or inexpensive pH testing for their customers. Once you know more about your soil, you can add organic matter and compost material to enhance it.

When the time comes to place your seeds or seedlings in the garden, carefully follow the directions provided on the package regarding distance and depth requirements. Overcrowded crops will not produce as well as those properly spaced. Also, pay attention to any suggested planting times. Some crops should be added to the soil early in the morning, while others adjust better when transplanted in the evening.

Maintain moisture in your kitchen garden and keep weeds to a minimum by adding mulch on the soil and around plants. Mulch also helps regulate the temperature of the soil in the garden beds. Organic mulches such as straw, newspaper, and grass clippings also break down over time and enrich the soil. There are a wide variety of store-bought and organic mulches from which to choose. Ideally, mulching should be done in the fall, early spring, and again a few weeks after planting new products in the garden. More may be added later in the season if necessary, especially if the weather in your area is warm and wet.

You may live in an area where growing a kitchen garden is not a feasible option, or for whatever reason you are unable to care for one of your own. That does not mean you can't enjoy the benefits of eating and cooking with organic and homegrown fruits, vegetables, and herbs. Look in your area for programs and cooperative organizations such as these:

- **Community supported agriculture (CSA):** CSAs enable individuals and families to purchase local, seasonal food items directly from farmers. The food usually includes a variety of vegetables but other farm products such as chesses and milks may be included. Information about programs and availability in your local region can be found at www.localharvest.org.

- **Community gardens:** Community gardens allow groups of people to collectively cultivate and produce fruits and vegetables on a designated piece of land. They are cropping up all across the nation. Visit www.communitygarden.org to learn more or find one in your vicinity.

- **Local farm stands and markets:** Buying produce and herbs from you local farm stand or market is yet another way to gain the benefits of fresh, local products while also supporting the agricultural community. It is wise to check with the owner about use of pesticides and other harmful chemicals on the food items. A comprehensive search of local farms, markets, and restaurants offering organic food is available through the Eat Well Guide (www.eatwellguide.org/i.php?pd=Home).

Basic pest and bug control will be necessary in your kitchen garden. Because most kitchen gardens are smaller and in raised beds, it should be fairly easy to keep control without the use of harmful chemical sprays. If you notice insects on your plants, handpick them off early in the morning when they are slower to react. A strong spray from a water hose will also wash away some bugs. Inviting frogs and snakes near or into your kitchen garden may also help keep bugs at bay. Interspersing plants like thyme, garlic, and chives among your crops will also deter or lure away some pests—a technique known as companion planting. If you have problems with bigger pests such as deer and rabbits, you may wish to consider installing fencing around your beds to protect your crops.

Although you will undoubtedly profit from the fresh air and exercise received while working the land, the greatest pleasure comes when it is time to harvest and eat the produce you grew in your kitchen garden. Avoid using items that appear overripe, damaged, or diseased and select only young, ripe plants. How and when to harvest will vary for each type of plant, so consult seed packets, catalogs, or your local nursery for specific details.

By harvesting fruits, vegetables, and herbs at their peak of ripeness, you will enjoy the maximum flavors, textures, and nutritional values they have to offer. Vitamins and minerals found in produce and herbs are most potent when they are freshest, so using them immediately will also bring the most benefits. Always harvest items the same day you intend to eat them, cook with them, or preserve them.

Helpful Books for Additional Reading

- *Great Garden Shortcuts* by Rodale Press
- *Kitchen Garden: How to create a beautiful and functional culinary garden* by Cathy Wilkinson Barash
- *Kitchen Garden: What to grow and how to grow it* by Lucy Peel
- *Rodale's Low-Maintenance Gardening Techniques* by Rodale Press
- *Square Foot Gardening: A new way to garden in less space with less work* by Mel Bartholomew

Chapter 3

Tips for
Canning &
Preserving

I t is possible for even a small kitchen garden to produce more crops than your family can consume at once. Instead of letting the abundance go to waste, many gardeners rely on methods of storing, canning, and preserving them for later use. Practicing simple food preservation techniques allows you to enjoy year-round use of homegrown items in your kitchen. Canning and preserving your garden's fruits, vegetables, and herbs will save you money on your grocery bill. More importantly, you and your family will be eating fresher and healthier foods. You can also maintain complete control over what goes into the items you serve and ensure they contain only the organically grown ingredients you choose.

Proper storage of your produce will help increase their longevity and quality. Produce, especially root vegetables (like carrots, beets, and potatoes), are often preserved by storing them in a small root cellar. A root cellar is basically any storage area that uses the earth's natural abilities to keep it insulated, humidified, and cool. One can be constructed as an attachment to your home, dug into a nearby hillside, or sometimes created in a cold basement. Well prepared and stored items should stay fresh throughout the winter months.

Basic Equipment Needed for Canning Fruits and Vegetables

Some equipment will vary slightly depending on what you are preparing, but here are a few standard items you will need to have on hand:

- Large stock pot or canner (pressure or water bath, depending on items you intend to can)
- Quart- or pint-sized canning jars (wide mouth jars work best) with lids and rings
- Canning funnel
- Tongs or jar lifter
- Large ladle or spoon

You may opt to preserve your items for longer storage by canning them. This process involves placing food in jars, heating them to kill micro-organisms that cause food to spoil, and then vacuum sealing them to prevent air from reentering the jars. Some items are simply canned in their natural form, while others are used to make pickles, sauces, or jellies. Examples of kitchen garden fruits and vegetables commonly used for canning are tomatoes, cucumbers, berries, and beans.

Safety Tips for Canning

- Use only jars specifically made for canning. Commercial jars are not thick enough and may break during the heating process.
- Sterilize jars before using. Running them through a complete cycle in the dishwasher will do the trick.
- To avoid burns or other kitchen incidents, never leave your canner unattended or handle hot jars without tongs or oven mitts. Always follow safety guidelines included with your pressure cooker.
- Make sure jars are properly sealed and labeled before storing.
- Store canned items in a cool, dry, and dark location (such as a cellar or pantry).
- Examine each jar closely before opening or using the contents. Do not ignore warning signs of possible spoilage or contamination such as bubbles, foam or leakage around the lid, a bulging lid, or unpleasant odor. Eating foods that are spoiled leads to botulism, a deadly form of food poisoning.

In addition to canning your fresh produce, you may also consider preserving some of your items by freezing or drying them. Many hearty vegetables and fruits like peppers, peas, and berries do well when properly frozen. Some items freeze better after a short boiling process, called blanching, which helps maintain their texture, nutritional value, and color. Herbs also do well in the freezer. Keep in mind that they will likely become mushier than when used fresh, but the flavor remains intact. Freezer-preserved herbs work well when used for cooking or making tea because the soggy texture will not impact the taste.

For long-term preservation of most herbs, drying is the preferred method. Herbs can be dried in several ways. For example, they can be quickly cooked in the microwave, slowly dried in a low heat oven, gathered in small bundles and hung to air dry, or dehydrated. Dried herbs should be labeled, stored in jars or airtight bags, and placed in a dark location. While drying is typically used for herbs, a few produce items such as hot peppers and garlic also store well when dried.

No-Can Homemade Refrigerator Pickles

These delicious refrigerator pickles are quick, easy and require no canning. Please note that because these pickles are not pressure sealed, they do need to stay refrigerated at all times. All you need to do is:

- Wash and slice your cucumbers (lengthwise for spears or cross-wise for bread-and-butter pickles).

- Heat 2 cups of vinegar and pickling mix to a near-boil. Place cucumbers in the sterilized jar, pour the simmering mixture over them, and seal the jar.

- Allow them to cool at room temperature, refrigerate for a few hours, and then wait. In a few days they are ready to eat.

Visit PickYourOwn.org for complete instructions (www.pickyourown. org/pickles_easy.htm)

Simple Strawberry Preserves

These simple strawberry preserves can be made in about an hour! Here is what you will do:

- Wash and chop your strawberries (about 6 cups) to the desired size.

- Add strawberries, sugar (4 cups), and a package of pectin to a large pot.

- Bring mixture to a boil, stirring continually to prevent sticking. Once boiling is complete, skim foam off the top.

- Allow the preserves to cool and seal. Then enjoy them on your favorite pastry or bread!

(Full recipe can be found at www.ehow.com/how_4995491_sensational-strawberry-preserves.html)

Breakfast

Katie's Apple Raisin Pancakes

(Courtesy of Chocolate-Covered Katie Blog: www.chocolatecoveredkatie.com)

Ingredients

¾ cup whole wheat flour
⅛ cup oats
2 tablespoons oat bran
½ teaspoon cinnamon
2 teaspoons baking powder
¼ teaspoon salt

¼ cup raisins
½ cup apple, chopped
1 cup apple juice or water

Directions

Combine the first six dry ingredients, then add the raisins and apple. Gently stir in the juice or water until the dry ingredients are completely moistened. Pour the batter by ¼-cupfuls onto a non-stick skillet or griddle. Cook until the bottoms are brown and a spatula can slip easily underneath. Turn and brown the other sides. Makes 8 pancakes.

Sweet Potato Pancakes

Ingredients

6 cups peeled and finely shredded sweet potatoes
1 cup finely shredded onions
1 teaspoon salt-free herb seasoning
1⅔ cup unbleached flour
⅓ cup chopped fresh flat-leaf parsley
2 cups finely shredded zucchini
¼ cup lemon juice
1 ½ cups egg substitute
6 teaspoons canola oil, divided

Directions

In a large bowl, mix the sweet potatoes, onions, herb seasoning, flour, parsley, zucchini, lemon juice, and egg substitute. In a large non-stick frying pan or griddle over medium-high heat, warm 2 teaspoons of the oil. Drop a large tablespoon of the batter into the pan and spread it with a spatula to form a thin pancake. Add more batter to fill the pan without crowding the pancakes. Cook for about 2 minutes per side, or until golden and crispy. Remove from the pan and keep warm. Repeat, adding the remaining 4 teaspoons of oil as needed, until all the batter has been used. Serve with Fruit Syrup (page 24).

Fruit Syrup

Ingredients

fresh or dried fruit
⅛ – ¼ cup sugar

Directions

Cook fresh fruit, or dried fruit that has been soaked in water, in a large quantity of water until it is very soft. Press through a strainer, reserving the syrup. It should be similar in consistency to ketchup. If not, add more hot water. For each cup of syrup, add ⅛-¼ cup of sugar, or sweeten to taste. Serve on Sweet Potato Pancakes (page 23).

Berry Blast Smoothie

Ingredients

2 cups blueberries
2 cups raspberries
2 cups strawberries
2 cups blackberries
1 cup 100% cran-raspberry juice
1 cup low-fat blueberry yogurt
2 cups ice

Directions

Place all items into blender and blend until smooth. Serve immediately.

Serves 8.

Nectarine and Basil Bagel

Ingredients

2 nectarines, thinly sliced
2 bagels, split
4 tablespoons fat-free cream cheese
12 large basil leaves
¼ teaspoon cracked black pepper

Directions

Toast bagels and spread with cream cheese (1 tablespoon per bagel half). Top with basil leaves and nectarine slices. Sprinkle with pepper.

Mad Scramble

(Courtesy of Chocolate-Covered Katie Blog: www.chocolatecoveredkatie.com)

Ingredients

⅓ block Mori-Nu firm silken tofu
⅔ tablespoon minced garlic
¼ teaspoon turmeric
½ teaspoon onion powder
two veggies (bell peppers, beech mushrooms,
baby bella mushrooms, tomatoes, zucchini, etc.)
salt and pepper to taste

Directions

Put the tofu in a pan and chop it up (not too finely, though).
Sprinkle the garlic and other seasonings on top of the tofu. Turn
the stove to medium-heat and sauté the tofu in whatever liquid you
prefer for sautéing (oil, water, vegetable broth, etc.). After about
10 seconds, add the vegetables. Stir constantly, and add water as
needed to prevent sticking. Cook until the vegetables are no longer
crisp (about 3-5 minutes).

Silken tofu is used in this recipe because the texture more closely
resembles that of scrambled eggs. You can also substitute with
eggs, is preferred.

Cantaloupe and Blueberry Parfait

Ingredients

6 tablespoons non-fat lemon
yogurt
¼ cup fat-free sour cream
2 cups cantaloupe, cubed
1 cup blueberries
4 mint sprigs

Directions

Mix yogurt and sour cream.

Layer ½ cup of cantaloupe, ¼ cup of blueberries, and 2 ½ tablespoons yogurt mixture in each of the glasses.

Garnish with a fresh mint sprig.

❚ This dish also makes a pretty brunch presentation!

Sweet Potato Pancakes with Apple-Walnut Topping

Ingredients

6 cups sweet potatoes or yams, shredded

¼ cup all-purpose flour

½ teaspoon baking powder

¼ teaspoon ground cinnamon

1 tablespoon honey

1 large egg

2 large egg whites

½ cup light brown sugar, firmly packed

⅓ cup walnuts, chopped

1 tablespoon orange juice

½ teaspoon ground cinnamon

Directions

Pancakes:

In a large bowl, combine sweet potatoes, flour, baking powder, cinnamon, honey, egg, and egg whites and stir with a fork until mixed well.

Coat a large non-stick skillet with cooking spray and place over medium heat. Drop the batter by about 2 tablespoonfuls into hot pan to make several pancakes. Flatten slightly with a spatula until about 3 inches across. Cook the pancakes until golden on both sides. Transfer the pancakes to a warm large plate and keep warm. Repeat with the remaining batter, coating the skillet with cooking spray, as needed.

Topping:

In a large skillet, stir together brown sugar, walnuts, orange juice, and cinnamon. Add the apples and cook over medium-high heat, stirring, until the apples are tender and the brown sugar has melted to form a syrup. Serve with the pancakes.

▌ McIntosh and Cortland apples are great for baking.

Zucchini Bread

(Courtesy of John Scheepers Kitchen Garden Seeds, www.kitchengardenseeds.com)

Ingredients

3 eggs
1 teaspoon vanilla
1 cup vegetable oil
2 cups sugar
1 teaspoon salt
2 teaspoons baking soda

¼ teaspoon baking powder
3 tablespoons cinnamon
2 teaspoons nutmeg
2 cups flour
2 cups grated zucchini
Optional: chopped walnuts, raisins or currants

Directions

Preheat oven to 350 °F. Grease and flour two loaf pans. With an electric mixer, whip the eggs until light and frothy. Add the vanilla and vegetable oil, reducing mixer speed so that it doesn't splatter everywhere. Gradually mix in the sugar until thick and well blended. Add the salt, baking soda, baking powder, cinnamon and nutmeg. Alternate adding the flour and the zucchini until all is incorporated. Add optional chopped walnuts, raisons or currents as you wish. Pour into the prepared pans, making sure that the batter only fills the pans two-thirds up otherwise it will overflow while baking. Bake at 350 °F for about one hour. If you are going to freeze them, let them get to room temperature, wrap in aluminum foil and then place in airtight freezer bags.

❚ Such a nice treat in the winter.

Yogurt Hang-up
with Strawberries

(Courtesy of John Scheepers Kitchen Garden Seeds, www.kitchengardenseeds.com)

In the Netherlands, "hangop" was an old-fashioned dessert made by "hanging up" a double-clothe sack filled with buttermilk overnight. The thickened buttermilk was then folded into thick whipped cream topped with brown sugar, cinnamon and crumbled "beschuit" (rusk). Here is our updated version that can be enjoyed for special breakfasts, healthy snacks or even dessert.

Ingredients

32 ounces low-fat plain yogurt
¼ cup wildflower honey
1 tablespoon orange zest
¾ cup seeded strawberry puree
2 teaspoons vanilla extract
strawberries, raisins, granola and wildflower honey for garnish

Directions

Line a strainer with a double thick layer of paper towels and position it over a bowl. Spoon the yogurt on top of the paper towels and cover it with plastic wrap. Refrigerate overnight. In the morning, you won't believe how much liquid has come out of the yogurt. (Discard the yogurt water.) Whisk the honey, orange zest, seeded strawberry puree and vanilla into the yogurt. Serve it in individual little bowls, topped with your favorite garnishes and drizzled with extra wildflower honey.

Soups

Summer Squash Bisque

This light summer soup can be served warm or chilled, and is great for using fresh zucchini and squash, both of which tend to harvest large amounts at once. It also sneaks in 2 cups of kale, a dark leafy green that is an amazing addition to a garden; it takes up very little space and grows continuously.

Ingredients

1 cup chopped shallots
½ cup chopped green onion
2 garlic cloves, minced
4 medium zucchini, chopped
2 small yellow summer squash, chopped
1 cup peeled and cubed Idaho potatoes

4 cups low-sodium vegetable broth
2 cups chopped kale
1 teaspoon dried tarragon
½ cup fat-free half and half
6 thin slices zucchini (for garnish)
6 thin slices yellow summer squash (for garnish)

Directions

Spray large saucepan with cooking spray; heat over medium heat until hot. Sauté shallots, green onions, and garlic until tender. Add chopped zucchini, yellow squash, and potato. Sauté for 5 to 8 minutes. Add stock, kale, and tarragon to saucepan; heat to boil and reduce heat to simmer. Cover until vegetables are tender (about 10 to 15 minutes). Process soup in food processor or blender until smooth and return to saucepan. Stir in half and half. Serve warm or chilled with a slice of zucchini and summer squash.

Gazpacho

▌ Nothing tastes better in gazpacho than ripe tomatoes right off the vine.

Ingredients

3 large tomatoes, quartered
2 cups cucumber, chopped
1 cup onion, chopped
1 cup green bell pepper, seeded and chopped
2 tablespoon red wine vinegar

2 teaspoons olive oil
1 clove garlic, chopped
1 cup water
salt and pepper to taste

Directions

Place tomatoes, cucumber, onion, bell pepper, vinegar, oil, and garlic in a food processor and process until desired consistency.

Place vegetable mixture in a serving bowl, add water and stir thoroughly.

Cover and refrigerate for at least 1 hour.

Add salt and pepper to taste.

Mushroom Soup

Growing edible mushrooms is actually very easy! Companies such as Fungi Perfecti (www.fungi.com) offer simple kits to grow your very own mushrooms safely.

Ingredients

¼ pound mushrooms
⅛ teaspoon pepper
3 cups stock
1 slice onion
2 tablespoons butter
1 cup hot milk

4 tablespoons flour
salt (optional)

Directions

Wash mushrooms, chops stems, simmer with stock and onion for twenty minutes, and press through a sieve, reserving two or three whole caps. Add milk, pepper, and salt (if desired). Thicken with butter and flour blended together. Cut mushroom caps into bits, and add to soup.

Vegetable Broth

Making a vegetable stock is a great way to use up any scraps of veggies that weren't used from other recipes.

Ingredients

3 quarts water
4-5 carrots
1 turnip
3-4 leeks, tied together in a bunch
1-2 cabbage leaves cabbage
1 onion
2 cloves (to be inserted into onion)

1 stalk celery
¼ pound butter
bouquet garni
salt and pepper, to taste

Directions

Place all ingredients into three quarts of water. Let boil gently for 3 hours. Pass broth through a strainer, and use as a base for various soups.

Broccoli Soup

Ingredients

3 cups chopped broccoli
(or 2 10-ounce packages frozen
broccoli)
½ cup diced celery
½ cup chopped onion
1 cup low-sodium chicken broth

2 cups non-fat milk
2 tablespoons cornstarch
¼ teaspoon salt
 dash pepper
 dash ground thyme
¼ cup grated Swiss cheese

Directions

Place vegetables and broth in saucepan. Bring to boil, reduce heat, cover, and cook until vegetables are tender (about 8 minutes). Mix milk, cornstarch, salt, pepper, and thyme; add to cooked vegetables. Cook, stirring constantly, until soup is lightly thickened and mixture just begins to boil. Remove from heat. Add cheese and stir until melted.

Curried Butternut Apple Soup

If there's an abundance of apples in your harvest, this soup is a unique way to present a snacking fruit. Depending on your harvest, try experimenting with sweet and tart apples to find which type flavors the soup to your taste!

Ingredients

¼ cup reduced-fat margarine
2 cups chopped onion
1 rib celery
4 teaspoons curry powder
2 medium butternut squash
(about 2 ½ – 3 lbs) peeled, seeded,
and cut into cubes

3 medium apples, peeled, cored,
and chopped
3 cups water (chicken stock or
vegetable broth)
1 cup cider

Directions

In a heavy kettle, combine onions, celery, margarine, and curry powder. Cover and cook over low heat until vegetables are tender (10–15 minutes), stirring often. Add cubed squash, chopped apples, and liquid (water, stock or broth) and bring to a boil. Reduce heat and simmer 20–30 minutes or until squash and apples are cooked thoroughly. Strain liquid and set aside. Puree the apple-squash mixture with one cup of the strained liquid. Add cider and remaining liquid to reach desired consistency. Garnish with grated apple, yogurt, or low-fat sour cream.

Beef and Bean Chili

(Courtesy of NHLBI, part of NIH and HHS)

Ingredients

2 pounds lean beef stew meat (trimmed of fat), cut in 1-inch cubes

3 tablespoons vegetable oil

2 cups water

2 teaspoons minced garlic

1 large onion, finely chopped

1 tablespoon flour

2 teaspoons chili powder

1 green pepper, chopped

2 pounds tomatoes, chopped (3 cups)

1 tablespoon oregano

1 teaspoon cumin

2 cups canned kidney beans

Directions

Brown meat in a large skillet with half of vegetable oil. Add water. Simmer covered for 1 hour until meat is tender.

Heat remaining vegetable oil in second skillet. Add garlic and onion and cook over low heat until onion is softened. Add flour and cook 2 minutes. Add the garlic-onion-flour mixture to the cooked meat. Then add the remaining ingredients to the meat mixture. Simmer for 30 minutes.

Broccoli Potato Soup

(Courtesy of the Massachusetts Department of Agricultural Resources)

This soup has a creamy base with less fat, and allows for the earthy flavors of your garden to come through.

Ingredients

3 medium potatoes, peeled
and diced
1 ½ cups fresh broccoli, chopped
½ medium onion, finely chopped
1 ½ cups water
3 cups skim milk

½ teaspoon pepper
¼ teaspoon garlic powder
½ cup cheese, grated

Directions

Bring water to a boil. Add vegetables and cook over medium heat until tender, about 15 minutes. Do not drain. Remove half of vegetables and mash. Return them to pot. Add milk, pepper, and garlic. Heat through. Serve with cheese sprinkled on top.

Serves 6.

Root Soup

(Courtesy of the Massachusetts Department of Agricultural Resources)

Ingredients

2 parsnips, scraped

2 carrots, scraped

½ cup barley

2 bouillon cubes

2 dashes Tabasco sauce

⅛ teaspoon curry powder

(optional)

4 small turnips, peeled

2 onions

6 cups water

1 tablespoon basil

pepper to taste

Directions

Grate turnips, parsnips, carrots and onions by hand or in a food processor. Put the grated vegetables in a large saucepan. Add the barley, water, bouillon cubes and basil and bring to a boil. Reduce the heat, cover and simmer for 1 to 2 hours. Check the soup often, add water as needed. Stir in the Tabasco sauce, pepper and curry.

Serves 10.

Leek and Potato Soup

(Courtesy of John Scheepers Kitchen Garden Seeds, www.kitchengardenseeds.com)

This soup is warming for a winter day, especially if you have potted up a sage plant to grow indoors. For a vegetarian version, omit the prosciutto. If not available, substitute bacon or ham.

Ingredients

¼ pound imported prosciutto, unsliced

1 pound leeks, trimmed, split and washed

1½ pounds red potatoes (with the skins on)

1 celeriac (celery root), about ½ pound after trimming and peeling

2 tablespoons butter

½ cup cream

2 tablespoons fresh sage, chopped (or 1 tablespoon dried)

1 large bay leaf

2 tablespoons chopped parsley

salt and freshly ground pepper

Directions

Cut prosciutto into ¼-inch cubes and sauté 5 minutes in a 4-quart saucepan over low heat. Remove with a slotted spoon and set aside. Melt the butter in the same pan, and cut the leeks into 1-inch pieces. Sauté the leeks in the butter over low heat for 10 minutes, being careful not to brown them. Cut potatoes and celeriac into ½-inch cubes, then add to the leeks along with the prosciutto, bay leaf and enough water to cover. Simmer slowly, uncovered, for about an hour, or until the vegetables are soft and the leeks have thickened the soup, adding more water if needed. Mash the cubed vegetables a bit while still in the pan, then add sage and cream. Add salt and pepper to taste and simmer for 2 minutes. Garnish individual servings with parsley.

Serves 4.

Dutch Cream of Mustard Soup

(Courtesy of John Scheepers Kitchen Garden Seeds, www.kitchengardenseeds.com)

A rich, wonderful meal all with a bit of bread, there is nothing quite like classic Dutch mustard soup. Unable to find a traditional recipe, we made up our own and hope that you enjoy its tangy bite and creamy texture.

Ingredients

6 tablespoons butter
1 leek, white part only, well rinsed, thinly sliced
1 yellow onion, chopped
1 carrot, peeled and sliced
1 shallot, minced
6 tablespoons flour
4 cups chicken stock, heated
1 ½ cups milk, scalded
bouquet garni (2 parsley sprigs, 3 bay leafs and 1 sprig fresh thyme)
½ cup heavy cream
2 egg yolks

1 cup chicken stock, heated
4 tablespoons Dutch mustard with whole mustard seeds (De Echte Zaanse Mosterd)
½ teaspoon white pepper
1 teaspoon salt
1 tablespoon snipped, fresh chive
½ cup creme fraiche
Optional: ½ pound green aspara-gus, lightly steamed, cut into 1-inch pieces and ⅓ pound Black Forest ham, sliced and cut into little pieces

Directions

Place the butter in a stock pot over medium heat. When melted, add the leek, onion, carrot and shallot. Sauté until the vegetables are soft, about 5 minutes. Add the flour and cook for 5 minutes while stirring to remove the taste of the flour.

Gradually stir in the hot chicken stock and hot milk. Add the bouquet garni, reduce the heat to low and simmer uncovered for about 45 minutes, stirring frequently. Strain the thickened soup into a clean soup pot, pressing the solids to extract as much liquid as possible. Add the cream and bring back to a simmer. Reduce the heat to low.

Whisk the egg yolks in a medium bowl. While whisking, slowly incorporate a ¼ cup of hot soup into the egg yolks. Incorporate another 1/2 cup of hot soup into the egg yolk mixture, whisking steadily. Then, incorporate a full cup of hot soup into the egg yolk mixture, whisking steadily. Return the egg yolk and soup mixture into the soup pot, whisking to blend. Thin the soup with the additional cup of heated chicken stock (more or less) to reach the desired thickness.

Over medium heat, bring the soup to just simmering. Whisk in the mustard, salt and pepper to taste. Add the creme fraiche, whisking until smooth. Optional: Add the drained, cut asparagus and pieces of ham. Serve piping hot, topped with chopped chives.

▌ For De Echte Zaanse Mosterd, check out www.alldutchfood.com.

Salads

Warm Spinach Salad

This light, warm salad is a perfect meld of sweet and tangy, and a whole new way to experience greens.

Ingredients

1 pound fresh spinach
2 teaspoons olive oil
6 red delicious apples
½ medium red onion
3 tablespoons balsamic vinegar
3 tablespoons olive oil
3 tablespoons toasted almonds,
sliced or slivered

Directions

Wash and de-vein spinach, removing all stems. Air dry spinach or put into salad spinner until dry.

Heat olive oil in large sauté pan or tilt skillet.

Halve apples lengthwise and cut into quarters. Remove cores. Slice into long thin slices.

Skin and slice onion in half. Slice into thin strips or julienne.

Add apples and onions to hot olive oil and sauté until slightly wilted and red onion begins to bleed.

Deglaze pan with balsamic vinegar, and remove from heat. Add remainder of olive oil and toss hot onion apple mixture into washed and dry spinach and toss well.

Serve immediately with garnish of toasted almonds.

Spinach Orange Salad

Ingredients

4 cups spinach, torn into pieces
2 medium oranges, sectioned
⅔ cup fresh mushrooms, sliced
½ cup red onion, sliced
2 tablespoons vegetable oil
2 tablespoons vinegar
¼ cup orange juice (from sectioning of orange)
½ teaspoon ground ginger
¼ teaspoon pepper

Directions

Place spinach in bowl. Add orange sections, mushrooms, and onion. Toss lightly to mix.

Mix oil, vinegar, orange juice, ginger, and pepper well. Pour over spinach mixture.

Toss to mix. Chill.

Confetti Coleslaw

Store-bought coleslaw can be soppy with dressing. Homemade is lighter, crunchier, and obviously more satisfying.

Ingredients

2 cups green cabbage, finely chopped
¼ cup green pepper, finely chopped
¼ cup red pepper, finely chopped
1 tablespoon onion, finely chopped

2 tablespoons vinegar
1 tablespoon water
1½ tablespoons sugar
⅛ teaspoon celery seed
⅛ teaspoon pepper

Directions

Mix vegetables together lightly. Mix remaining ingredients together for dressing.

Stir dressing into vegetables. Chill well.

Coriander Crusted Scallop Salad with Orange Tarragon Vinaigrette

(Courtesy of Busch's Fresh Food Market)

Ingredients

2 tablespoons orange juice concentrate

1 tablespoon white balsamic vinegar

3 tablespoons extra-virgin olive oil

1 teaspoon sea salt, divided

1 head Boston (or bibb) lettuce, chopped

2 tangerines, sectioned

1 cucumber, peeled and thinly sliced

¼ cup chopped fresh tarragon

2 tablespoons ground coriander seeds

1 tablespoon coarsely crushed black peppercorns

1½ pounds sea scallops

Directions

Preheat the grill on high heat or preheat broiler. Whisk juice concentrate, vinegar, 2 tablespoons of the olive oil and ½ teaspoon of the salt in a bowl; set aside.

Combine lettuce, tangerines, cucumber and tarragon in another bowl; set aside.

Rub scallops with the remaining tablespoon of olive oil and sprinkle with remaining ½ teaspoon salt and ground coriander.

Place the scallops on an oiled broiler pan or thread onto skewers. Grill or broil scallops, turning occasionally, until no longer translucent, about 6-7 minutes total.

Toss salad greens mixture with dressing and divide between 4 plates; divide the scallops evenly between the plates

Mixed Greens Salad with Edamame, Oranges and Asparagus

(Courtesy of Busch's Fresh Food Market)

Edamame is the Japanese name for fresh soybeans. Edamame are a lovely green color and are occasionally available fresh. Frozen beans, shelled or in the pod, are delicious and more readily available. Mixed baby greens, such as mesclun, may be substituted.

Ingredients

1 teaspoon minced shallots
1 tablespoon white wine vinegar or orange flavored vinegar
2 teaspoons Dijon mustard
3 tablespoons walnut or almond oil
1½ teaspoons orange zest
1 cup shelled frozen edamame
18 thin asparagus spears, ends snapped

4 cups mixed organic greens, washed and spun dry
2 cups red leaf lettuce, washed and spun dry
2 navel oranges, peeled and sectioned (zest used above)
kosher salt and freshly ground pepper

Directions

Soak shallots in vinegar for 30 minutes.

Whisk together oil, orange zest and shallot mixture. Season to taste with salt and pepper. Let stand an additional 30 minutes.

Bring a large pot of salted water to a boil. Cook edamame about 5 minutes. Remove with a slotted spoon; rinse under cold water and set aside. Add asparagus to water, cook 3 minutes or until just tender. Remove and immediately immerse in ice-cold water. Drain and set aside.

Meanwhile, arrange mixed greens and red leaf lettuce on a large platter or individual plates. Arrange asparagus and orange wedges over greens. Drizzle with dressing, sprinkle edamame over salad and serve.

Savory Salad

Letting this jarred salad sit in the fridge before serving will allow the flavors to meld. It's very similar to pickling cucumbers!

Ingredients

1 quart raw cabbage, chopped
1 quart cooked beets, diced
½ cup grated horseradish
2 cups brown sugar
1 tablespoon salt
vinegar

Directions

Mix all the ingredients (except vinegar). Add enough vinegar to cover. Place in a covered jar. Use when desired. Serve on lettuce leaves.

Sweet and Sour Leafy Green Salad

Ingredients

5 cups torn and lightly packed romaine lettuce leaves
3 cups lightly packed spinach leaves
2 cups sliced mushrooms
2 oranges peeled and sliced
1 cup halved pitted prunes

½ cup sliced red onion
½ cup non-fat honey mustard dressing
¼ teaspoon coarsely ground black pepper

Directions

Toss all ingredients in a large bowl.

Turkey Waldorf Salad

Waldorf salad is often served as a light dessert, but with the addition of turkey it's perfect for lunch.

Ingredients

2 cups sliced celery
2 cups diced unpeeled sweet apples
2 cups diced cooked turkey breast (12 ounces)
¼ cup sliced green onions
2 cups cooked small shell pasta
½ cup walnuts, coarsely chopped and toasted

Yogurt Dressing:
½ cup plain non-fat yogurt
3 tablespoons reduced-calorie mayonnaise
3 tablespoons cider vinegar
1 tablespoons sugar
⅛ teaspoon ground black pepper

Directions

In large bowl, combine celery with pasta, turkey, apple, scallions and walnuts. (To toast walnuts, place in small dry skillet over low heat until golden brown, about five minutes, stirring occasionally.) Blend all yogurt dressing ingredients together. Add dressing to salad and gently mix thoroughly.

Makes 7 cups.

Crunchy Carrot Salad

(Courtesy of the Massachusetts Department of Agricultural Resources)

Low in sodium, this salad will more than meet your daily vitamin A requirement.

Ingredients

1 ½ cups fresh, grated carrots
1 unpeeled red apple, chopped
¼ cup raisins
⅛ cup toasted slivered almonds (optional)
½ cup low-fat plain yogurt

1 ½ tablespoons low-fat mayonnaise
2 teaspoons lemon juice
salad greens

Directions

Combine carrots, apple, raisins, and almonds in a salad bowl. Blend together remaining ingredients in a separate bowl and add to carrot mixture. Serve on salad greens.

Serves 3.

Italian Basil Tomato Salad

(Courtesy of the Massachusetts Department of Agricultural Resources)

Ingredients

4 medium fresh tomatoes
5-6 fresh basil leaves, chopped
2 tablespoons vegetable oil
3 tablespoons wine vinegar
salt and pepper to taste

Directions

Cut the tomatoes in thin wedges or slices and spread them out in a wide, shallow bowl. Combine remaining ingredients and sprinkle over tomatoes. Baste the tomatoes with the dressing by tilting the dish and spooning it over the tomatoes repeatedly. Marinate 20-30 minutes before serving.

Serves 4.

Faith's Chopped Salad

(Courtesy of John Scheepers Kitchen Garden Seeds, www.kitchengardenseeds.com)

Faith Ohms helped her husband, Jan, start the Van Engelen flower bulb company some 35 years ago as she raised four daughters and taught painting classes. An acrylic artist specializing in large, trompe d'oeil paintings of vegetables, flowers and more recently, animals, Faith whips together meals without recipes, letting her creative spirit move her in (and out of) the kitchen

Ingredients

1 head Grappa or
Merveille lettuce
4 plum tomatoes
2 cups diced Holland European
cucumber
1 cup chopped celery
1 large sweet red pepper
1 cup pitted, drained ripe olives
½ cup finely chopped red onion

1 cup crumbled gorgonzola cheese

Dressing:
1 cup light mayonnaise
1 cup plain, low-fat yogurt
1 cup ketchup
¼ cup herbed vinaigrette
Maggi seasoning
salt and pepper to taste

Directions

Wash, dry, and tear the lettuce into very small pieces. Wash, seed and cut the plum tomatoes and red pepper into very small pieces. Layer all ingredients in a large, glass salad bowl, starting with the lettuce on the bottom. Just before serving, toss salad well and dress lightly to taste with her special dressing.

Dressing:

Whisk together the mayonnaise, yogurt, and ketchup in a medium bowl. Add your favorite herbed vinaigrette (we prefer Hopkin's Inn House Dressing) to lighten the consistency and add Maggi seasoning (an old Dutch favorite) and salt and pepper to taste.

Fish & Seafood
Entrées

Asparagus with Sole

Ingredients

1 pound asparagus
1 pound Sole fillets (4 pieces approximately the same size)
¼ teaspoon salt
½ teaspoon grated lemon or lime peel

4 tablespoons lemon or lime freshly squeezed juice
⅛ teaspoon black pepper
1 tablespoon finely chopped chives
1 teaspoon mustard

Directions

Cut asparagus into 3-inch lengths. Cook in 2-quart saucepan in lightly salted water for 5 minutes, drain. Set aside. Season the skin side of the sole fillets with salt and lemon or lime peel. Place asparagus spears at one end of each fillet. Roll up fillets with asparagus spears inside and secure with plain round toothpicks. Place in a 2-quart oven-safe casserole dish liberally sprayed with non-stick cooking spray. In a small bowl combine remaining ingredients and pour over fish. Bake in a 400 °F oven for approximately 15 to 20 minutes or until fish flakes easily. Baste fish every 7 minutes.

Soba Peanut Noodles with Shrimp

Soba noodles and edamame give this dish a Japanese flair, but the peanut sauce and cilantro are common in Thai cooking.

Ingredients

8 ounces soba noodles
or whole-wheat spaghetti
¼ cup natural crunchy peanut
butter
4 cups shredded cabbage
2 cups shredded carrots
1 cup edamame, shelled and
thawed

1 tablespoon grated fresh ginger
2 garlic cloves, minced
½ cup chicken broth
1 pound shrimp, peeled and uncooked
2 tablespoons Hoisin sauce
2 teaspoons chili sauce
or 1 teaspoon red chili paste
¼ cup chopped cilantro (optional)
non-stick cooking spray

Directions

Cook noodles. Drain and rinse. Set aside in large mixing bowl.

In a small saucepan, combine garlic, ginger, chicken broth, peanut butter, hoisin sauce, and chili sauce. Cook on low heat stirring until peanut butter is blended.

Spray non-stick spray in large frying pan. Add cabbage, carrots, and edamame. Cook for about 5 minutes.

Add shrimp and sauce mixture and cook until shrimp turn pink, about 5 minutes.

Pour mixture over noodles and mix until noodles are well coated.

Top with fresh cilantro (optional) and serve.

Serves 6.

Spanish Paella

This Spanish-inspired rice dish includes shrimp and lots of vegetables. Try this one-dish meal that's ready in minutes.

Ingredients

2 tablespoons olive oil
1 medium onion, diced
1 clove garlic, minced
1 cup rice (dry)
1 cup diced red pepper
¾ cup diced zucchini
2½ cups low-sodium chicken broth

¾ cup frozen peas, thawed
1¾ cups tomatoes, chopped
1 (15 oz.) can chickpeas, rinsed and drained
1 pound peeled shrimp
⅛ teaspoon salt
⅛ teaspoon pepper
⅛ teaspoon saffron

Directions

Heat olive oil in oven-safe large skillet. Add garlic and onion. Stir for 3 minutes on medium heat.

Add rice, red pepper, zucchini, and ½ cup of chicken broth. Stir for another 5 minutes.

Add remaining ingredients except shrimp. Stir and place skillet in the oven.

Bake at 375 °F for 20 minutes. Add shrimp. Cook until shrimp turns pink, about 5 minutes. Serves 4.

If you don't have saffron on hand, use yellow rice. Look for it next to other rice varieties in the grocery store.

You can make this recipe vegetarian by using vegetable broth

Scandinavian Baked Halibut Dinner

Ingredients

1 ½ pounds halibut fillets or steaks

1 tablespoon all-purpose flour

3 tablespoons juice of 1 large lemon

2 tablespoons dry white wine

12 cherry tomatoes

12 small white new potatoes, steamed

3 tablespoons fresh dill, chopped

grated zest (½ of lemon)

1 tablespoon margarine, melted

lemon wedges, for serving

freshly ground white or black pepper

Directions

Preheat oven to 425 °F. Cut the halibut into 4 equal pieces. Lightly coat the fish with the flour, shaking off the excess; season with pepper.

Coat a large non-stick skillet (preferably ovenproof) with cooking spray and place over medium-high heat. Add the fish and cook for about 2 minutes on each side. If the skillet is not ovenproof, transfer the fish to a 2-quart shallow baking dish.

Sprinkle the fish with the lemon juice and wine. Place the tomatoes and potatoes around the fish and sprinkle with 2 tablespoons of the fresh dill or 1 teaspoon dried.

Bake, uncovered, for about 10 minutes, or until the fish is opaque throughout. Sprinkle the fish with the remaining dill and the lemon zest. Drizzle the margarine over the potatoes. Serve with lemon wedges, if desired.

Curried Shrimp in Carrot Nest

It sounds exotic, but this quick and easy dish using 5 basic ingredients and a few common extras is a showstopper with color, presentation, and flavor.

Ingredients

2 cups carrots, coarsely shredded or julienne

1 extra large onion, chopped to yield 2 cups; reserve 2 tablespoons

1 ½ tablespoons sugar

1 tablespoons water

2 tablespoons olive oil or cooking oil

2 large cloves garlic, peeled and chopped

1 pound peeled medium shrimp (may be frozen)

2 to 3 teaspoons mild curry powder (if spicier is desired, use hot curry powder)

2 tablespoons flour

1 cup low-sodium chicken broth

1 tablespoon non-fat yogurt

1 tablespoon lime juice

1 tablespoon chopped parsley

2 cups cooked rice tossed with ½ cup cooked peas and 2 tablespoons chopped peanuts (optional)

salt and pepper (optional)

Directions

Place shredded carrots, 2 tablespoons chopped onion (only) and sugar in a medium-sized skillet with 1 tablespoon water; heat on high to boiling, covered. Cook for 1 to 2 minutes, until carrots are barely done. Remove immediately and cool. Reserve. Prepare optional rice suggestion and reserve if desired. Heat oil in large deep skillet on medium-high heat. Add garlic and peeled shrimp and sauté until shrimp are opaque and tender. Remove shrimp from skillet and set aside. To remaining oil in pan, add curry powder and remaining chopped onion. Sauté over medium heat until onions are transparent, coated with curry flavor and somewhat caramelized. Add flour and stir until flour disappears. Add chicken broth and stir continuously until onion curry sauce has thickened. Stir in yogurt, lime juice, and cooked shrimp. Season with salt and pepper if desired.

To serve:

Warm carrots briefly in pan. Place optional rice mixture in large circle on serving plate. Arrange warm carrots inside the ring, leaving a space directly in the center for the curried shrimp. Garnish with chopped parsley. Serve immediately.

Garden State Seafood Panzanella Salad

Ingredients

8 littleneck clams
4 large sea scallops
3 ounces calamari
3 ounces monkfish
½ cup large diced tomato
½ cucumber, julienne (match stick size) or preferably cut on a mandolin to resemble spaghetti
¼ fennel bulb, julienne (reserve a few fronds for garnish)

4 basil leaves, roughly chopped
3-4 whole basil leaves for garnish
1 scallion, cut on the bias into thin slices (reserve the green top for garnish)
½ cup extra virgin olive oil
2 garlic cloves, sliced
1 cup water
3 teaspoons lemon juice
1 large baguette
½ teaspoon sea salt
black pepper to taste

Directions

Bread:

Remove the crust from the bread and cut into ½-inch cubes. Lightly toast the bread in a 350 °F oven and set aside. You will need about ½ cup of toasted bread cubes for the recipe. The rest of the bread can be used for the optional garnish described below if desired.

Vegetables:

Cut the tomato into large dice. Dice the cucumber and fennel into matchstick size pieces (julienne). Slice the garlic cloves. Cut the scallions into small slices on the bias. Roughly chop the basil (chiffonade). Reserve some scallion tops and fennel fronds for garnish. Keep all of this chilled until ready to use.

Seafood:

Skin the monkfish and cut into bite size pieces. Rinse the clams of any sand.

Peel the abductor muscle from the sides of the sea scallops. Peel and clean the squid, pull the tentacles and all that are attached from out of the tube. Cut the tentacles off just above from where they start and discard the beak and eyes. Also remove the tough clear membrane from within the tube and discard. Slice the squid into ¼ inch rings. Keep all of the seafood well chilled until ready to prepare. Heat a large frying pan and add the olive oil. Season the scallops and monkfish with salt and pepper and sear them until browned on the outside, remove from the oil and reserve on a plate on the side. Add the garlic and let brown slightly, add the calamari and give a quick toss. Next add the clams and the water, season lightly with salt and pepper. Cover until the clams begin to open and then return the scallops and monkfish to the pan. Cook covered until all the clams open. Try adding more water if clams do not open after 1- 2 minutes and adjust liquid to assure you have about ½ cup of liquid left when the dish is finished. Discard any unopened clams.

To assemble:

Put the cut vegetables into a large bowl with the basil and season with salt and pepper. Add the bread cubes and toss with the vegetables. Just before serving toss in the hot seafood and half of the cooking liquid. Portion onto plates, garnish with the scallion sprigs and fennel fronds and pour the remaining seafood broth around each plate. Serve immediately.

Optional garnish:

Make toasted bread ring molds by taking a large baguette and slicing it lengthwise into ¼ inch slices. Grease metal ring molds with olive oil and wrap the bread around them. Tie with kitchen string and bake until golden brown in a hot 350 ˚F oven. Remove from the oven, let cool, remove the string and carefully remove the bread from the molds. You can put these in the center of your plate and fill with some of the salad for an impressive presentation. Also garnish with the fennel fronds, scallion top and fresh basil leaves.

Grilled Baja-Style Fish Tacos

Ingredients

1 tablespoon olive oil
2 tablespoons fresh lime juice, divided
1 pound swordfish steak or other hearty white fish fillets (such as halibut or cod)
½ cup chopped fresh cilantro
¼ cup reduced–fat or regular sour cream

¼ cup light mayonnaise
1 jalapeño, seeded and finely chopped
8 (6-inch) corn tortillas
1 cup shredded cabbage or coleslaw mix
1 tomato, chopped
salt and freshly ground black pepper

Directions

In a shallow plate, combine oil and 1 tablespoon lime juice. Add fish, turning to coat, and marinate for 15 minutes. Preheat a lightly oiled grill to medium-high. Remove fish from marinade and sprinkle with salt and pepper. Grill fish for 4 to 7 minutes per side, or until cooked through. Remove from grill and let rest for 5 minutes before slicing into ⅓ to ½-inch thick pieces. Meanwhile, in a bowl, combine cilantro, sour cream, mayonnaise, jalapeño, and the remaining 1 tablespoon lime juice. Wrap the tortillas in a damp paper towel and warm in the microwave on high for 15 to 30 seconds. Top each tortilla with cabbage, sour cream mixture, and fish. Sprinkle with tomatoes.

Spinach Stuffed Sole

(Courtesy of NHLBI, part of NIH and HHS)

Fresh spinach makes all the difference in this recipe. Frozen and thawed spinach cannot even compare.

Ingredients

1 teaspoon olive oil
½ pound fresh mushrooms, sliced
½ pound fresh spinach, chopped
¼ teaspoon oregano leaves, crushed
1 clove garlic, minced

1½ pounds sole fillets or other white fish
2 tablespoons sherry
4 ounces (1 cup) part-skim mozzarella cheese, grated
non-stick cooking spray

Directions

Preheat oven to 400 °F.

Spray a 10 x 6-inch baking dish with non-stick cooking spray. Heat oil in skillet; sauté mushrooms about 3 minutes or until tender. Add spinach and continue cooking about 1 minute or until spinach is barely wilted. Remove from heat; drain liquid into prepared baking dish. Add oregano and garlic to drained sautéed vegetables; stir to mix ingredients.

Divide vegetable mixture evenly among fillets, placing filling in center of each fillet.

Roll fillet around mixture and place seam-side down in prepared baking dish.

Sprinkle with sherry, then grated mozzarella cheese. Bake 15-20 minutes or until fish flakes easily. Lift out with a slotted spoon.

Scallop Kabobs

(Courtesy of NHLBI, part of NIH and HHS)

Ingredients

3 medium green peppers, cut into
1 ½-inch squares
1 ½ pounds fresh bay scallops
1 pint cherry tomatoes
¼ cup dry white wine
¼ cup vegetable oil

3 tablespoons lemon juice
dash garlic powder
black pepper to taste

Directions

Parboil green peppers for 2 minutes. Alternately thread first three ingredients on skewers.

Combine next five ingredients. Brush kabobs with wine/oil/lemon mixture, place on grill (or under broiler). Grill 15 minutes, turning and basting frequently.

Dilled Fish Fillets

Ingredients

1 pound frozen haddock or cod fillets
1 tablespoon lemon juice
⅛ teaspoon dried dill weed
⅛ teaspoon salt
dash of black pepper

Directions

Thaw frozen fish in refrigerator overnight or thaw in microwave oven. Then, separate into 4 filets or pieces. Place fish in a glass-baking dish. Cover with wax paper. Cook at medium power in the microwave for 3 minutes. Remove cover, turn fish over, and sprinkle with lemon juice and seasonings. Cover and continue cooking over medium heat for 3 minutes or until fish flakes with a fork.

Skillet method:

Separate into four fillets or pieces. Place fish in heated fry pan. Sprinkle with lemon juice and seasonings. Cover and cook over medium heat until fish flakes when tested with a fork, about 5 minutes.

Butternut Squash Shrimp Bisque

(Courtesy of John Scheepers Kitchen Garden Seeds, www.kitchengardenseeds.com)

The sweet, creamy texture and flavor of butternut squash make this bisque velvety-rich without the addition of too much cream. If preferred, vegetable stock may be used in place of chicken stock and blanched asparagus spears may be floated in place of shrimp. So nice in front of a crackling fire with a crusty baguette.

Ingredients

½ cup sweet butter
1 cup diced onions
½ cup all-purpose flour
5 ½ cups chicken stock
5 cups diced and peeled butternut squash (about 3 pounds)

1 cup dry white wine
3 bay leaves
1 cup whipping cream
1 pound small, uncooked, peeled and cleaned shrimp
salt and freshly ground pepper to taste

Meat & Poultry Entrées

Chicken Ratatouille

(Courtesy of NHLBI, part of NIH and HHS)

Ingredients

1 tablespoon vegetable oil
12 ounces boneless, skinless chicken breast, cut into thin strips
2 zucchini, about 7 inches long, unpeeled, thinly sliced
1 small eggplant, peeled, cut into 1-inch cubes
1 medium onion, thinly sliced
1 medium green bell pepper, rinsed and cut into 1-inch pieces

½ pound fresh mushrooms, rinsed and sliced
2 whole peeled tomatoes, chopped
½ tablespoon garlic, minced (about 1 clove)
1½ teaspoon dried basil, crushed
1 tablespoon fresh parsley, rinsed, dried, and minced
⅛ teaspoon ground black pepper

Directions

Heat oil in a large non-stick pan. Add chicken, and sauté for about 3 minutes or until lightly browned.

Add zucchini, eggplant, onion, green pepper, and mushrooms. Cook for about 15 minutes, stirring occasionally.

Add tomatoes, garlic, basil, parsley, and black pepper. Stir and continue to cook for about 5 minutes. Serve warm.

Chicken and Quinoa

(Courtesy of Busch's Fresh Food Market)

Quinoa is a complete protein grain, making this meal as healthy as it is filling.

Ingredients

1 tablespoon extra virgin olive oil
8 chicken thighs, skin removed
1 large onion, diced small
3 cups seeded, diced Roma tomato
2 large cloves of garlic, minced
1 cup low sodium chicken broth
4 tablespoons fresh lime juice
2 teaspoons dried thyme

2 teaspoons dried ground cumin
1 teaspoon salt
½ pound diced zucchini or yellow squash
1 cup quinoa, rinsed and drained
freshly ground black pepper

Directions

Heat the olive oil in a large deep non-stick skillet. Pat the chicken thighs dry and brown them on both sides in the skillet, working in batches if necessary. This will take about 3-4 minutes per side.

Remove the chicken from the pan and place on a plate. Add the onions to the pan and sauté for five minutes or until lightly browned. Add the tomatoes and garlic to the pan and bring to a simmer.

Return the chicken to the pan and add the chicken broth, lime juice, thyme, cumin and salt. Cover and simmer for 15 minutes.

Add the zucchini or yellow squash and quinoa to the pan. Cover the pan and simmer on low until the quinoa is fluffy and soft. Add black pepper to taste and serve.

Scalloped Potatoes with Turkey Bacon

Ingredients

4 medium potatoes
½ pound turkey bacon
flour
salt, used sparingly
pepper
milk

Directions

Pare the potatoes and cut them into thin slices. Cook the turkey bacon until brown, and cut each slice into several pieces. Oil a baking dish and place a layer of potatoes in it, then a layer of turkey bacon. Sprinkle with flour, salt, and pepper. Repeat until all the ingredients are used, the top layer should be turkey bacon. Add milk until it reaches the top layer. Bake on medium heat for one hour, or until much of the milk has evaporated and the potatoes are tender. Serve hot.

Sesame Chicken with Peppers and Snow Peas

Ingredients

1 tablespoon sesame seeds
1 pound boneless, skinless chicken breast, cut into strips
2 cups snow peas, trimmed
1 large red bell pepper, cubed
1 large green bell pepper, cubed
3 tablespoons low-sodium soy sauce

2 tablespoons water
1½ teaspoons brown sugar
¼ teaspoon ground ginger
2 green onions, sliced
non-stick cooking spray

Directions

Place sesame seeds in a large non-stick skillet. Cook 2 minutes over medium-high heat until lightly browned. Remove from skillet and set aside. Spray same skillet with non-stick cooking spray. Add chicken. Cook for 10 minutes or until chicken is cooked through. Add snow peas and bell peppers; stir-fry for 3 to 4 minutes until vegetables are crisp and tender. In a small bowl, combine soy sauce, water, brown sugar, and ginger; add to skillet. Cook for 5 minutes over medium-high heat. Sprinkle with green onions and serve.

Chicken Tortas

Ingredients

3 cups Pico de Gallo (page 123)
2 cups cooked, shredded chicken, without skin
1 teaspoon chili powder
2 cups chopped romaine lettuce
4 thin white onion slices

2 large radishes, sliced
½ cup shredded low-fat Monterey Jack cheese
4 Bolillo or French rolls, cut in half lengthwise

Directions

Prepare the Pico de Gallo (page 123). In a medium bowl, combine chicken, chili powder and 1 cup of Pico de Gallo. Reserve the other 2 cups of Pico de Gallo. In a second bowl, combine lettuce, onion, radishes, and cheese. Place equal amounts of chicken and lettuce mixtures inside of each roll. Spoon ¾ cup of the Pico de Gallo over the lettuce in each sandwich. Close the sandwich.

Serves 4.

Cosmic Cucumber Wrap

Ingredients

1 ounce lean ground beef
1 tablespoon onion, chopped
1 cup Romaine lettuce, shredded
¼ cup fresh tomatoes, diced
¼ cup cucumber, diced
1 (8-inch) whole wheat tortilla
1 tablespoon fat-free ranch salad dressing

Directions

Brown ground beef and onion in skillet over medium heat, drain excess fat. Mix lettuce and tomato together with ground beef mixture. Chop cucumber and mix with salad dressing. Place tortilla on a plate and spread with beef mixture. Top with cucumber and salad dressing mixture and roll wrap.

Balsamic Chicken Salad

Ingredients

⅓ cup balsamic vinegar
1 tablespoon Dijon mustard
¼ teaspoon seasoned salt
¼ teaspoon sugar
⅛ teaspoon black pepper, freshly ground
12 ounces boneless, skinless chicken breast halves

1 pound sweet onion, cut into 12 wedges
8 cups (6 ounces) mixed baby salad greens
2 cups seedless grapes
2 tablespoons fresh basil, thinly sliced

Directions

Preheat grill to medium-high. In a small bowl, whisk together the vinegar, mustard, salt, sugar, and pepper until blended and smooth. Pour 2 tablespoons of the dressing into a cup and brush over the chicken and onion wedges. Let the chicken and onion stand for 5 minutes.

Grill the chicken for 12 to 15 minutes, or until a thermometer inserted in the thickest portion registers 160 ºF and the juices run clear, turning once. Grill the onion for 3 to 5 minutes on each side, or until soft. In a large bowl, toss together the salad greens, grapes, basil, and the remaining dressing until evenly coated; transfer to a platter. Cut the chicken into ½-inch thick slices and arrange over the salad.

Prosciutto-Wrapped Asparagus

Great for a light lunch or dinner, this is the perfect way to cook and serve asparagus. The prosciutto is what takes it from a simple vegetable side dish to an elegant main course.

Ingredients

2 garlic cloves, unpeeled
1 tablespoon olive oil
1½ ounces mild fresh goat cheese
¼ teaspoon pepper
16 asparagus spears, trimmed
4 paper-thin prosciutto slices
1 clove garlic, minced

2 tablespoons chopped fresh cilantro
1 tablespoon cider vinegar
½ teaspoon ground cumin
1 teaspoon vegetable oil

Directions

Preheat oven to 400 °F. Place garlic cloves in small baking dish. Drizzle olive oil over garlic; toss to coat. Bake until garlic is very soft, basting occasionally with oil, about 15 minutes. Pour oil off, place garlic into small bowl. Cool garlic and peel. Add garlic, goat cheese and pepper to oil and mash together.

Cook the asparagus spears by placing on parchment paper on a cooking sheet, drizzle with olive oil and salt and bake at 400 °F for 8 minutes. Wrap four spears in each prosciutto slice. Arrange on a plate and spoon the garlic-cheese over the top.

Creamy Tomato, Bacon and Blue Cheese Linguine

(Courtesy of John Scheepers Kitchen Garden Seeds, www.kitchengardenseeds.com)

Ingredients

1 tablespoon butter
2 tablespoons chopped shallots
1 ½ teaspoons chopped garlic
1 ¼ cups heavy cream
2 tablespoons fresh parsley
¼ teaspoon fresh oregano

½ teaspoon fresh basil
peeled, seeded and chopped plum
tomatoes (about 4 cups)
12 ounces linguine
4 chopped bacon slices
¼ cup fresh cilantro
1 cup grated Parmesan cheese
⅓ cup crumbled blue cheese

Directions

Melt butter in large saucepan over medium heat. Add shallots and garlic, sauté till translucent, about 2 minutes. Stir in cream and chopped parsley, oregano and basil. Simmer till sauce is reduced to one cup, about 3 minutes.

Fry bacon in large, heavy skillet over medium-high heat till crisp. Drain all but 1 tablespoon drippings from pan. Add tomatoes, chopped cilantro and cream sauce; simmer till heated through, about 3 minutes. Combine ½ cup Parmesan cheese and ⅓ cup blue cheese in small bowl. Add by handfuls to sauce mixture and stir till melted. Season to taste with salt and pepper.

Cook linguine in large pot of boiling, salted water till almost tender, stirring occasionally. Drain pasta. Add to sauce and toss to coat. Transfer to large bowl. Sprinkle pasta with remaining ½ cup Parmesan cheese and serve.

Savory Chicken Roll-ups

(Courtesy of John Scheepers Kitchen Garden Seeds, www.kitchengardenseeds.com)

We love to capture the summer's harvest in special entrees that freeze well for cozy, winter dinners with friends. A personal favorite, this one is a bit time consuming but is well worth it!

Ingredients

Filling:
1 tablespoon butter
½ cup chopped onions
1 clove minced garlic
½ cup chopped mushrooms
2 chopped pieces prosciutto
3 diced artichoke bottoms
1 pound chopped, cooked spinach
1 cup cooked rice
8 boned chicken breast halves
seasoned flour
extra butter
herbs to taste

Sauce:
3 tablespoons oil
3 tablespoons butter
½ cup chopped onions
1 clove minced garlic
1 cup chopped mushrooms
¼ cup chopped celery
⅜ cup chopped carrots
2 tablespoons flour
½ cup white wine
1 cup chicken stock
1 tablespoon tomato paste
⅛ teaspoon thyme
2 bay leaves

Directions

Preheat oven to 375 °F.

Filling:

Sauté onions in butter for 3 minutes. Add garlic and mushrooms; cook for 2 minutes. Add remaining filling ingredients. Add herbs to taste: salt, pepper, tarragon, fines herbs. Set aside. Pound chicken breasts till thin. Place one tablespoon filling on each breast. Roll and tie with cooking string. Dredge in seasoned flour. Chill for 30 minutes or overnight.

In skillet, brown roll-ups in butter for 5 minutes and place in casserole dish.

Sauce:

Sauté onions, garlic, mushrooms, celery and carrots in butter. Add flour and cook until golden. Add white wine, chicken broth and tomato paste, stirring until smooth. Add thyme, bay leaves, salt and pepper to taste. Pour sauce over chicken roll-ups in casserole. Cook covered for 30 minutes. Serve with long grain and wild rice. Makes 8 roll-ups.

Braised Beef Brisket with Savory Root Vegetables

(Courtesy of John Scheepers Kitchen Garden Seeds, www.kitchengardenseeds.com)

Wintry Sunday afternoons are made for roasted chickens or braised beef roasts so that their aromas may be savored. It's also fun to feel like a pioneer, pulling homegrown root vegetables out of our "cold room" and snipping fresh herbs from kitchen pots as the snows fly and the winds howl.

Ingredients

1 fennel bulb
4 large carrots
2 pounds rutabagas
4 large parsnips
2 pounds red-skinned potatoes
3 tablespoons olive oil
3 chopped onions
4 cloves minced garlic
1 ½ cups dry red wine
3 ½ cups beef broth
2 tablespoons tomato paste

1 tablespoon paprika
½ teaspoon ground ginger
½ teaspoon allspice
3 bay leaves
1 tablespoon sage chiffonade
4 teaspoons fresh thyme leaves
paprika
1 (4 ½ pound) boneless beef brisket
sea salt
freshly ground black pepper
parsley sprigs

Directions

Cut fennel bulb, carrots, rutabagas, parsnips and potatoes into 1½-inch slices. Preheat oven to 325 °F.

Heat olive oil in heavy skillet over medium heat. Add chopped onions and minced garlic. Sauté for 10 minutes until golden, stirring. Add red wine, beef broth, tomato paste, 1 tablespoon paprika, ginger, allspice, bay leaves, thyme and sage chiffonade (thinly cut ribbons). Bring to boil, simmer for 10 minutes. Pour broth into large Dutch oven. Rub paprika on all sides of beef brisket. Put brisket fat side up in the broth bath. Cover, bake for 1 hour.

Arrange root vegetable slices around the brisket. Cover. Bake for 2 ½ hours more until brisket is tender. Remove from oven. Transfer brisket to cutting board to rest the meat for 15 minutes. In batches, pour cooking liquid into blender to puree with some of the vegetables, reserving the majority of the vegetables aside in a large bowl. Pour pureed sauce into heavy saucepan: boil for 10 minutes until reduced to 3 ½ cups. Season with salt and pepper. Thinly slice brisket across grain and arrange on a platter surrounded by root vegetables and drizzled with sauce. Garnish with fresh parsley and serve with extra sauce.

Serves 8.

Vegetarian
Entrées

Warm Lentils with Fennel and Arugula

(Courtesy of Busch's Fresh Food Market)

Ingredients

1cup French lentils

1 teaspoon kosher salt

1 fresh fennel bulb (medium to large)

1 tablespoon olive oil or walnut oil

3 garlic cloves minced or pressed

2 teaspoons crushed fennel seeds

1 ½ teaspoons dried thyme

4 cups fresh arugula, chopped

⅓ cup chopped toasted walnuts

Directions

Bring the lentils, 3 cups of water and ½ teaspoon of salt to a simmer. Cook covered 20-25 minutes until lentils are tender but not mushy.

Meanwhile core and slice the fennel into thin strips (about 2 cups).

In a large skillet, heat oil and sauté garlic for 1 minute. Add ground fennel and thyme and stir for a couple seconds. Add fresh fennel and the other ½ teaspoon salt and sauté for 2-3 minutes or until fennel begins to get softened but is still crisp. Remove from heat.

When the lentils are done, drain and add them to the fennel and escarole mixture along with the walnuts.

Brilliant Couscous with Black Beans and Roasted Red Peppers

(Courtesy of Busch's Fresh Food Market)

Ingredients

1 cup dried black beans, rinsed
1 large red pepper
4 teaspoons ground cumin
¼ cup fresh lime juice
2 tablespoons olive oil
½ teaspoon turmeric
1 cup water or chicken stock
1 cup whole wheat couscous

1 teaspoon salt
½ cup thinly sliced green onions
⅓ cup chopped fresh cilantro
1 ½ teaspoons minced chipotle chilies

Directions

Stir 3 teaspoons of the cumin in small dry skillet over medium heat just until fragrant, about 1 minute. Remove from heat. Whisk lime juice and oil into skillet. Pour the dressing out of the skillet into a measuring cup or bowl.

Stir the turmeric and remaining cumin in heavy, medium sized saucepan over medium heat until fragrant, about 1 minute. Add 1 cup of water or chicken stock and salt. Bring the mixture to a boil and add the couscous. Cover the pan and immediately remove it from the heat.

Cool couscous to room temperature. Mix onions and half of dressing into couscous. Season with salt and pepper.

Combine black beans, roasted red peppers, cilantro, chipotle chilies, and remaining dressing in medium bowl. Toss to coat. Season with salt and pepper.

Mound bean mixture in center of platter. Surround with couscous salad. Serve with sliced avocado and your favorite salsa.

Caribbean Bean Salad

Ingredients

4 cups chopped Romaine lettuce
¼ cup red onion
1 cup canned black beans, drained and rinsed
1 orange, peeled and diced
1 tomato, diced

1 tablespoon olive oil
3 tablespoons red wine vinegar
1 teaspoon dried oregano
black pepper to taste

Directions

In a large salad bowl, toss all ingredients together. Serve immediately or refrigerate up to 1 hour.

Serves 4.

Roasted Radishes and Root Vegetables

Roasted veggies are tasty, and very easy to prepare! As an added bonus, tonight's leftover roasted veggies can be part of tomorrow's lunch—just add them to a salad, soup or sandwich. Try serving this recipe with cold pasta to create a delicious pasta salad.

Ingredients

3 medium sweet potatoes, peeled and cut into 2-inch chunks (about 3 cups)
4 medium parsnips, peeled and cut into 2-inch chunks (about 2 cups)
2 medium red onions, peeled and quartered

1 whole head garlic, cut in half
12 ounces radishes, scrubbed
2 ½ tablespoons olive oil
¼ teaspoon salt
½ teaspoon black pepper
1 tablespoon fresh or 1 teaspoon dried thyme

Directions

Preheat oven to 450 °F. In a large bowl, mix the potatoes, parsnips, onions, radishes and garlic. Toss with olive oil, salt and pepper. Arrange vegetables in a single layer in a 15 ½" x 10 ½" roasting pan. Be sure the oven is fully heated before placing the pan in the oven. Bake until vegetables are fork tender and golden (about 45 minutes), stirring occasionally. Arrange vegetables on a serving platter. Squeeze the garlic cloves out of their skins. Sprinkle with salt and pepper. Garnish with thyme sprigs.

Serves 4.

Bow Tie Pasta with Roasted Garlic and Eggplant

Ingredients

12 ounces bow tie pasta, uncooked
2 tablespoons fresh parsley (or 1 tablespoon dried parsley)
4 tablespoons olive oil
½ cup balsamic vinegar
¼ teaspoon dried oregano

½ teaspoon ground pepper
6 cups eggplant, peeled and cut into 1-inch cubes
3 cups chopped tomato (about 3 medium tomatoes)
1 bulb garlic
¼ cup grated Parmesan cheese

Directions

Preheat oven to 375 °F. Cut off the pointy tip of the garlic head to expose the garlic cloves inside. Wrap in foil. Bake 1 hour or until very soft. Unwrap and allow garlic to cool. To use the garlic, squeeze each clove toward the cut end to collect the soft flesh.

In medium bowl, mix 3 tablespoons olive oil, vinegar, oregano, pepper, and eggplant. Marinate in the refrigerator for 1 hour. Place eggplant mixture, with liquid, in a baking pan. Bake in a preheated 425 °F oven for 25 minutes. Stir every 5 to 6 minutes.

Cook pasta in a pot of boiling water according to the package instructions. Drain pasta and divide among 6 serving plates. About 10 minutes before eggplant is completely cooked, heat 1 tablespoon olive oil in a skillet. Add tomatoes and roasted garlic. Sauté 5 minutes.

Top the pasta with roasted eggplant; then, tomato-garlic mixture; and finally, with parsley. Serve immediately sprinkled with Parmesan cheese.

Spaghetti Squash

Ingredients

1½ cups baked spaghetti squash (see box)
1 teaspoon Dijon mustard
1½ tablespoons vegan mayo
⅛ cup water
garlic salt to taste
Optional: Try mixing corn and/or chopped brussels sprouts and nutritional yeast into the squash

Directions

Mix all the ingredients (except the squash and optional ingredients) in a cup. Then pour over the squash and stir. Add optional ingredients if you wish. Eat cold.

Serves 1.

How to Prepare Spaghetti Squash
1. Poke a few holes into the squash with a knife.
2. Cut in half, and place the halves right side up on a piece of tin foil.
3. Bake the squash in a (not pre-heated) 405 °F oven for about 1 hour.
4. Microwave for about 2-3 minutes.
6. Scoop out the insides. For a more caramelized taste, mix with salt and spices, then put under the broiler for a few minutes. Otherwise, just eat it with whatever sauce you want (or just plain).

Spinach Pesto Pasta

Pesto sauce and cannellini beans are popular in many Italian dishes. No one will know that this pesto sauce has three cups of spinach.

Ingredients

8 ounces fettucine

1 tablespoon olive oil

1 garlic clove, minced

3 cups fresh spinach, stems removed

1 cup fresh basil leaves, stems removed

½ cup chicken broth, low-fat, low-sodium

¼ cup grated Parmesan cheese

1 (15 oz.) can cannellini (white beans), rinsed and drained

1 cup red bell pepper, chopped

1 teaspoon black pepper

Directions

Cook pasta as directed on package. Drain and place in large mixing bowl.

In a blender, add olive oil, garlic, spinach, basil, Parmesan cheese, and chicken broth. Mix well until leaves are blended.

Pour sauce over pasta. Mix until pasta is well coated.

Add beans and red bell pepper. Lightly toss and serve.

Make extra pesto and freeze for later use.

Need a quick side? Cook pasta or rice. Heat pesto sauce. Toss and serve.

Try using diced tomatoes instead of bell peppers or chickpeas instead of white beans.

Chickpea and Spinach Curry

▌ Curry powder gives this dish a taste of India. Serve over brown rice.

Ingredients

1 cup onion, coarsely chopped
1½ tablespoons fresh ginger,
chopped or grated
1 teaspoon olive oil
1½ teaspoons curry powder
1 (19 oz.) can chickpeas, rinsed
and drained
1 ¾ cups tomatoes, chopped

1 ¼ cups fresh spinach, stems
removed
½ cup water
¼ teaspoon salt (optional)

Directions

Combine onion and ginger in food processor and pulse until
minced.

Heat oil in large skillet over medium-high heat.

Add onion mixture and curry. Sauté 3 minutes.

Add chickpeas and tomatoes; simmer for 2 minutes.

Stir in spinach, water, and salt. Cook another minute until spinach
wilts.

Serves 6.

▌If you don't have a food processor, chop onion and ginger into
small pieces.
Try with other beans, such as navy beans, black-eyed peas, or
lentils instead of chickpeas. These beans should be cooked before
using in this recipe.

Leafy Tofu

Ingredients

1 (20 oz.) package tofu
3 cups spinach leaves, fresh
2 tablespoons soy sauce, low-
sodium
1 teaspoon toasted sesame seeds
non-stick cooking spray

Directions

Drain tofu and cut into 1-inch cubes. Tear spinach into bite-sized pieces. In a large pan, spray with cooking spray and sauté tofu cubes for a few minutes. Move tofu to the center of the pan. Add spinach and soy sauce. Mix. Cover pan and cook until spinach is wilted. Sprinkle with toasted sesame seeds.

Grilled Eggplant Tomato Sandwiches

▌ A meatless sandwich that is immensely satisfying.

Ingredients

1 medium Italian eggplant, cut
into ½-inch slices
1 tablespoon salt
1 ½ tablespoons olive oil
2 cloves garlic, crushed
3 tablespoons finely minced fresh
basil

8 (½-inch) slices crusty bread
4 medium ripe tomatoes
freshly ground black pepper
½ cup crumbled Feta cheese
(optional)

Directions

Do not peel eggplant. Remove end and cut into ½-inch slices.
Sprinkle both sides with salt and allow to rest for 10 minutes.
Thoroughly rinse slices to remove all salt and drain on absorbent
paper.

Combine olive oil and garlic and lightly brush each slice. Grill over
medium-high heat on gas grill or broil under broiler. When soft,
remove immediately and sprinkle with basil.

Meanwhile, slice tomatoes into slices and season with black pepper.
Arrange tomatoes and eggplant on 4 slices of bread. Season with
pepper and add crumbled Feta cheese, if desired. Top with second
slice of bread and serve immediately.

Squash with Tomato-Garlic Sauce

Ingredients

1 large spaghetti squash, cut in half lengthwise
½ tablespoon olive oil
5 medium firm, ripe tomatoes, peeled, seeded, and chopped
1 clove garlic, crushed with the side of a chef's knife

¼ cup balsamic vinegar
¼ cup reduced-fat Parmesan cheese, freshly grated
½ cup basil leaves, lightly packed, cut into thin strips
ground black pepper and salt (optional)

Directions

Preheat oven to 350 °F. Wrap the squash halves in aluminum foil and place in a baking dish. Bake for 45 minutes, or until tender. Reduce oven temperature to 200 °F. Meanwhile, in a large skillet, heat oil over medium heat. Add tomatoes and garlic and cook, stirring, for 20 to 30 minutes, or until the mixture thickens. Add vinegar and season with salt and pepper, if desired. Carefully open the foil (be careful of any steam) and remove squash. Scoop out the seeds and discard. With a large spoon, scoop the stringy flesh into a bowl. Using two forks, pull apart the flesh so it separates into spaghetti-like strands. Transfer the spaghetti squash to a serving dish. Spoon the tomato sauce over the squash and sprinkle with Parmesan and basil.

Fresh Vegetable Pita Pizza

Ingredients

1 pound fully ripened fresh
tomatoes
4 (7-inch) pita breads
1 tablespoon olive oil
2 tablespoons grated Parmesan
cheese
1½ teaspoons Italian seasoning,
divided

2 cups shredded part-skim mozzarella cheese, divided
1 medium zucchini cut in half
lengthwise and thinly sliced
(about 2 cups)
½ large green bell pepper, cut in
half lengthwise and thinly sliced
(about 1 cup)
¼ cup thinly sliced sweet red or
white onion

Directions

Preheat oven to 425 ºF. Core and slice tomatoes; cut each slice
in half. Place pitas on 2 baking sheets; brush with oil. Arrange
tomato slices on each pita, dividing evenly. Sprinkle with Parmesan
cheese and half of the Italian seasoning. Bake until tomatoes
are heated and pitas begin to crisp, about 10 minutes. Sprinkle
tomatoes with half of the mozzarella cheese. Top with zucchini,
green pepper and onion. Sprinkle with remaining mozzarella and
Italian seasoning. Bake until cheese is melted and vegetables are
crisp-tender, about 10 minutes. Serve with crushed red pepper, and
additional Parmesan cheese, if desired.

Eggplant Potato Crust Pizza

Ingredients

Flat bread:
1 russet potato
1 tablespoon olive oil
¼ teaspoon salt
1 ½ cups flour
1 egg

Topping:
1 eggplant, lightly grilled and thinly sliced
4 Roma tomatoes, thinly sliced
5 large basil leaves, roughly chopped

1 (8 oz.) ball of fresh mozzarella, thinly sliced
1 teaspoon crushed red pepper flake
salt and pepper to taste

Sauce:
1 tablespoon olive oil
1 (8 oz.) can whole, peeled tomatoes
1 tablespoon chopped basil
¼ teaspoon dried oregano

Directions

Puree all sauce ingredients and simmer on stove top over medium heat for 10 minutes, then let stand.

Bake the potato until it is tender, then cool in the fridge. Preheat your oven to 500 °F. Once the potato is cool, peel it and mash the pulp. Mix in olive oil, salt, flour and egg and blend well.

Let the dough sit at room temperature for 10 minutes to rest. Press dough onto an oiled pizza pan. Lightly sprinkle the dough with salt and pepper and add the crushed red pepper.

Next, spread sauce on the dough and place an even layer of eggplant, tomatoes and cheese on top of the dough. Top by sprinkling with crushed basil.

Bake the pizza in oven for approximately 15 minutes or until the crust is golden brown. Cut and serve.

Side Dishes

BBQ Lentils

Ingredients

12 ounces barbeque sauce
3 ½ cups water
1 pound dry lentils
2 green peppers, diced
2 red peppers, diced
2 small onions, diced
1 clove garlic, minced

Directions

Combine all ingredients in slow cooker. Cover and cook on low for 6-8 hours.

Variations:

Save time and bake this recipe. Sauté red peppers, green peppers, and garlic for 5 minutes. Add lentils and stir for another 5 minutes. Mix lentils, peppers, garlic, barbeque sauce, and 1 cup water in a glass baking dish. Bake at 375°F for 60 minutes.

Cauliflower Mashed Potatoes

This is a great way to try something different with cauliflower, especially if eating it raw or steamed is getting tiresome or isn't to your liking.

Ingredients

1 head cauliflower
1 teaspoon minced garlic
2 tablespoons plain yogurt
2 teaspoons butter
1 tablespoon Parmesan cheese (optional)
salt and pepper to taste

Directions

In a saucepan, steam cauliflower and garlic for 20-25 minutes, or until very tender. Immediately transfer the cauliflower to a food processor and add in yogurt, butter, and Parmesan (if desired). Process in short bursts, until it resembles mashed potatoes (process in small portions if necessary). Add salt and pepper to taste.

Veggie Rice Pilaf

Ingredients

¼ cup chopped carrot
⅓ cup chopped celery
¼ cup chopped bell pepper
½ cup chopped onion
2 cups chicken broth
1 tablespoon margarine
1 cup rice
¼ teaspoon black pepper

Directions

Preheat oven to 350 °F.

Wash carrots, celery and green peppers. Discard inedible portions, and chop edible portions.

Cut onion in half and remove ends. Peel one half of the onion, and chop this half.

Bring broth to a boil in saucepan.

Combine boiling broth and margarine in 1-quart casserole dish, and stir until melted.

Stir in rice, chopped vegetables, and black pepper.

Cover and bake at 350 °F for 35 minutes or until rice is tender and liquid is absorbed.

Remove from oven and let stand, covered, for 5 minutes. Fluff with fork, and serve.

Caribbean Pink Beans

(Courtesy of NHLBI, part of NIH and HHS)

Ingredients

1 pound dried pink beans
2 medium plantains, finely chopped
1 large tomato, rinsed and finely chopped
1 small red bell pepper, rinsed and finely chopped
1 medium white onion, finely chopped
1½ tablespoons garlic, minced (about 3 cloves)
1½ teaspoons salt

Directions

Rinse and pick through beans for rocks and other debris (discard these). Put beans in a large pot, and add 10 cups of water. Place pot in refrigerator, and allow beans to soak overnight.

Place the soaked and drained beans in a large pot with enough water to cover them by about 1 inch. Boil gently with lid tilted until beans are soft, about 1 hour. Add more water while beans are cooking if water level drops below the top of the beans.

Add plantains, tomato, red pepper, onion, garlic, and salt. Continue cooking at low heat until plantains are soft. Serve warm.

Roasted Beets with Orange Sauce

(Courtesy of NHLBI, part of NIH and HHS)

Often thrown into salads, beets hardly get to stake claim as a full-fledged side dish. This unique dish showcases the beautiful color of a root vegetable and doesn't skimp on flavor in the process.

Ingredients

1½ pounds small beets, leaves trimmed, each peeled and cut into four chunks
1 teaspoon olive oil
1 orange, rinsed
(for peel and juice)
½ teaspoon anise seeds (optional)

Directions

Preheat oven to 450 °F. Cover a baking sheet with aluminum foil for easy cleanup.

In a medium bowl, toss the beets with the olive oil until well coated.

Spread beets on baking sheet in a single layer.

Bake 30–40 minutes. When done, beets should be easily pierced with a sharp knife.

While beets bake, grate the zest from the orange. Place in a small bowl. Cut the orange in half. Squeeze the juice (about ½ cup) into the bowl with the orange zest. (Use a large spoon to press the inside of the orange to extract more juice.) Add anise seeds (optional). Set aside.

When the beets are tender, return them to the tossing bowl. Pour the juice mixture over the beets. Mix well to coat, and serve.

Asparagus with Lemon Sauce

(Courtesy of NHLBI, part of NIH and HHS)

▌ Try this lemon sauce over other vegetables as well!

Ingredients

20 medium asparagus spears, rinsed and trimmed
1 fresh lemon, rinsed (for peel and juice)
2 tablespoons reduced-fat mayonnaise
1 tablespoon dried parsley
⅛ teaspoon ground black pepper
¹⁄₁₆ teaspoon salt

Directions

Place 1 inch of water in a 4-quart pot with a lid. Place a steamer basket inside the pot, and add asparagus. Cover and bring to a boil over high heat. Reduce heat to medium. Cook for 5–10 minutes, until asparagus is easily pierced with a sharp knife. Do not overcook.

While the asparagus cooks, grate the lemon zest into a small bowl. Cut the lemon in half and squeeze the juice into the bowl. Use the back of a spoon to press out extra juice and remove pits. Add mayonnaise, parsley, pepper, and salt. Stir well. Set aside.

When the asparagus is tender, remove the pot from the heat. Place asparagus spears in a serving bowl. Drizzle the lemon sauce evenly over the asparagus (about 1½ teaspoons per portion) and serve.

Sunshine Rice

(Courtesy of NHLBI, part of NIH and HHS)

Ingredients

1½ tablespoons vegetable oil
1¼ cups celery, with leaves, rinsed
and finely chopped
1½ cups onion, finely chopped
1 cup water
½ cup orange juice

2 tablespoons lemon juice
dash hot sauce
1 cup instant white rice, uncooked
¼ cup slivered almonds

Directions

Heat oil in a medium-sized saucepan. Add celery and onion, and
sauté until tender (about 10 minutes).

Add water, juices, and hot sauce. Bring to a boil over high heat.

Stir in rice, and bring back to a boil. Cover and turn heat down
to simmer until rice is tender and liquid is absorbed, about 5–10
minutes.

Stir in almonds. Serve immediately.

Saffron Infused Chickpeas and Potatoes

(Courtesy of Busch's Fresh Food Market)

Ingredients

2 cups dried chickpeas
2 tablespoons extra virgin olive oil
2 teaspoons minced fresh garlic
½ cup diced onion
2 teaspoons ground cumin
1 teaspoon smoked Spanish paprika
1 teaspoon ground cinnamon

½ teaspoon ground black pepper
¼ teaspoon ground cayenne pepper
¼ teaspoon crushed saffron threads
½ teaspoon kosher salt
2 tablespoons tomato paste
1 pound diced unpeeled redskin potato
1 tablespoon lemon zest

Directions

Heat the olive oil in a heavy, deep skillet, or saucepan. Add the garlic and sauté for one minute. Add the onions and sauté for 3-4 minutes or until the onions begin to brown and soften.

Add the cumin, paprika, cinnamon, ground pepper, cayenne, saffron, salt, and tomato paste and sauté for one minute. Add the drained chickpeas and the diced potato and sauté until they are coated with spices.

Add the reserved liquid from the chickpeas and bring it to a simmer. Add the lemon zest, reduce the heat to low, cover the pan and simmer until the potatoes are tender and most of the liquid has been absorbed. This will take 45 to 60 minutes.

Adjust the seasonings with additional salt if necessary and serve.

Grilled Corn on the Cob

Ingredients

4 ears fresh corn, with silks and husks
1 fresh lime or lemon, cut into wedges
salt, pepper, chili powder to taste (optional)

Directions

Leave on husks and silks, and soak corn for 30 minutes in enough water to cover. Remove corn from water and pull the husks away from the top of the cobs to drain any excess water. Pull husks back over the cobs. Place corn on grill over hot coals and close lid of grill. Cook 25–30 minutes, turning frequently, until corn is tender. Remove corn from grill. If husks are too hot to handle, let them cool before removing husks. Squeeze fresh lemon juice over corn. Sprinkle with salt, pepper, or chili powder. Serves 4.

Soulful Greens

This version of the popular Southern dish uses orange juice for sweetness and red pepper flakes for spice. Serve with black-eyed peas and BBQ chicken, two other Southern favorites.

Ingredients

½ cup low-sodium chicken broth
¾ cup water
2 pounds collard greens, washed and stems removed
1 ½ cups red onions, sliced
1 garlic clove, minced
¼ cup orange juice
½ teaspoon dried red pepper flakes

Directions

Heat chicken broth and water in a large pot. Bring to a boil. Add collards and cook for 10 minutes.

Sauté garlic and onions for 5 minutes in a skillet.

Add orange juice and wilted greens. Stir until well coated. Simmer for 5 minutes.

Sprinkle with red pepper flakes and serve. Serves 4.

Soak collard greens in water to remove dirt and grit. Rinse until the water is clear.

Can't find collard greens? Try this recipe with mustard greens, kale, spinach, or broccoli rabe.

Zesty Skillet Zucchini

Ingredients

½ cup tomato juice, low-sodium
¼ teaspoon black pepper
1 onion, medium
1 tomato, medium
1 cup mushrooms, canned, rinsed
and drained

2 zucchini, medium
1 teaspoon basil

Directions

Peel and chop the onion into small pieces. Chop the tomato. Drain
and rinse the mushrooms. Cut zucchini into small slices. Place the
tomato juice and pepper in a skillet or pan. Cook on medium heat
for 3 minutes. Add the onion, tomato, and mushrooms. Reduce
the heat to medium-high. Cover and cook for 5 minutes. Add the
zucchini. Cover and cook for another 5 minutes.

Corn on the Cob with Lime Butter

▌ Kick up the rich flavor of sweet corn with lime and chili!

Ingredients

4 tablespoons salted, light margarine
1 teaspoon grated lime peel
1 tablespoon fresh lime juice
1 teaspoon chili seasoning
4 ears yellow corn-on-the-cob, fresh and in the husk

Directions

Combine margarine with lime peel, juice and chili seasoning. Mix until all the juice has been incorporated into the margarine. Cover and allow to stand for at least 30 minutes. Remove outer leaves of the corn husk, leaving inner leaves. Remove as much silk as possible. Rinse in cold water and place all 4 ears in plastic storage bag. Close the bag, leaving about 1-inch unsealed.

Place corn in microwave and cook on high for 6 minutes. Carefully turn bag over and cook on high for 4 more minutes. Remove carefully. Cool briefly, peel remaining husk and silk. Serve hot with 1 teaspoon chili lime butter for each serving.

Honey-Roasted Parsnips

Ingredients

1 ½ cups parsnips, peeled and cut into bite-sized chunks
1 large sweet potato, peeled and cut into bite-sized chunks
2 firm Gala or Fuji apples, peeled, cored and cut into bite-sized chunks

1 tablespoon canola oil
1 tablespoon honey
1 tablespoon balsamic vinegar
canola oil spray

Directions

Preheat oven to 375 °F. Coat a casserole dish with canola oil spray and set aside.

In a large mixing bowl, place the parsnips, sweet potatoes and apples and set aside.

In a microwave-proof bowl, mix together the canola oil and honey. Place in a microwave and warm for 10 seconds. Mix in balsamic vinegar. Pour onto vegetables and apples. Toss to coat well. Transfer to casserole dish, cover and bake until tender, about 1 hour.

Dips

Applesauce

(Courtesy of the Massachusetts Department of Agricultural Resources)

Ingredients

6 apples (or 4 apples and 2 pears)
½ cup water
¼ teaspoon cinnamon

Directions

Wash, peel, and cut fruit into small pieces. Discard core. Put apple pieces in a saucepan. Add only enough water to cover the bottom of the pan. Place saucepan on burner and bring water to boil. Turn heat down to a simmer and cover. Stir occasionally until apples are soft. Turn off heat. Mash apples and add cinnamon. Serve warm or cold.

Serves 4.

Baba Ghanoush (Eggplant Dip)

Ingredients

2 large eggplants (1 ¼ pounds)
2 tablespoons tahini
4 cloves garlic, peeled and crushed
3 tablespoons fresh lemon juice or more to taste
4 tablespoons cold water
¼ teaspoon salt
⅛ teaspoon freshly ground black pepper

½ teaspoon olive oil
1 cup chopped tomato
½ cup diced onion
parsley sprigs to garnish (optional)

Directions

Pierce the eggplants in several places with a toothpick or fork. Wrap each eggplant in aluminum foil and place on a gas grill or in the oven at 500 °F. Cook until the eggplants collapse and begin to release a lot of steam, about 10-15 minutes. Remove the foil and place the eggplants into a bowl of cold water. Peel while eggplants are still hot and allow them to drain in a colander until cool. Squeeze pulp to remove any bitter juices and mash the eggplant to a puree. In a food processor, mix tahini, garlic, onion, tomato, lemon juice, and water until mixture is concentrated. With the blender running, add the peeled eggplant, salt, pepper, and olive oil. Serve in a shallow dish and garnish with black pepper, tomatoes, and parsley.

Cantaloupe Salsa

This is a fun spin on salsa! It's also a great way to show off sweet, ripe cantaloupe.

Ingredients

½ large ripe cantaloupe
¾ cup finely diced red bell pepper
¼ cup finely chopped cilantro
3 tablespoons finely chopped scallions
juice of 1 lime
pinch salt and hot pepper flakes

Directions

Remove seeds and rind from cantaloupe. (You should have approximately ½ pound cantaloupe flesh.) Chop cantaloupe into very small diced pieces. Put in diced cantaloupe into a bowl. Add diced red pepper, cilantro, scallions and lime juice. Stir. Add pinch of salt and pepper flakes. Chill. Serve with grilled chicken, fish or steaks.

Caribbean Watermelon Salsa

When seed-spitting contests get old while the watermelon harvest is still very much young, try a sweet and spicy salsa with flavors to take you out of your garden and into the Caribbean.

Ingredients

2 cups watermelon, chopped and seeded
1 cup chopped fresh pineapple
1 cup chopped onion
¼ cup chopped fresh cilantro
¼ cup orange juice
1 tablespoon jerk seasoning

Directions

In large bowl, combine all ingredients; mix well. Refrigerate, covered, at least one hour to blend flavors. Stir before serving.

Watermelon Salsa

(Courtesy of Chocolate-Covered Katie Blog: www.chocolatecoveredkatie.com)

Ingredients

3 cups seedless watermelon, diced
¼ cup lime juice
¼ cup red onion, minced
salt to taste
Optional: 1 or 2 jalapeño peppers

Directions

Stir all the ingredients together and chill.

Cucumber Yogurt Dip

Lots of fresh veggies always need a creamy dip. While many store-bought vegetable dips are heavily cream-based, ours is made with yogurt, and uses fresh cucumber to make it even lighter. It's so easy to make (and eat!) with fresh ingredients.

Ingredients

2 cups plain low-fat yogurt
2 large cucumbers, peeled, seeded, and grated
½ cup non-fat sour cream
1 tablespoon lemon juice
1 tablespoon fresh dill

1 garlic clove, chopped
1 cup cherry tomatoes
1 cup broccoli florets
1 cup baby carrots

Directions

Peel, seed, and grate one cucumber. Slice other cucumber and set aside. Mix yogurt, grated cucumber, sour cream, lemon juice, dill, and garlic in a serving bowl. Chill for 1 hour. Arrange tomatoes, cucumbers, broccoli, and carrots on a colorful platter. Serve with cucumber dip.

Tomato Ketchup

Try baking fries from garden potatoes and serving them with homemade ketchup. Adjust the seasonings to taste for a slightly sweeter or tart ketchup.

Ingredients

12 ripe tomatoes
2 large onions
4 green peppers
2 tablespoons salt
4 tablespoons brown sugar
2 tablespoons ginger

1 tablespoon cinnamon
1 tablespoon mustard
1 nutmeg, grated
1 quart vinegar

Directions

Peel the tomatoes and onions. Finely chop the onions and peppers. Cook all the ingredients together for 3 hours, or until soft and broken. Stir frequently. Bottle and seal while hot.

Pico De Gallo

Ingredients

1 pound ripe tomatoes, chopped
1½ cups chopped onion
⅓ cup chopped fresh cilantro
3 jalapeño peppers, seeds removed and chopped
2 tablespoons lime juice
2 cloves garlic, minced
¼ teaspoon salt

Directions

Combine all ingredients in a medium bowl. Serve immediately or cover and refrigerate for up to 3 days.

Makes 6 servings (½ cup per person).

Hummus with Garlic and Lemon

(Courtesy of Lauren Sudekum)

Ingredients

1 can garbanzo beans
¼ cup vegetable broth
2 cloves garlic
¾ fresh lemon juice
2 tablespoons extra virgin olive oil
1 tablespoon finely minced fresh herb
(such as parsley, basil, or thyme)
salt and pepper to taste

Directions

Heat the vegetable broth to medium in a medium-sized, shallow pan. Rinse the garbanzos in a colander and pour into the broth. Heat until broth has evaporated, about 5-8 minutes. Test the beans with a fork for tenderness about halfway through. Once the broth has evaporated they should mash easily. If they're still hard, heat for a few extra minutes with a few additional tablespoons of broth.

Balsamic Cippolini

(Courtesy of Emily Teel)

Ingredients

8-10 fresh cippolini onions
1 ½ tablespoons extra virgin olive oil
2 tablespoons sugar
¼ cup vegetable broth
2 tablespoons balsamic vinegar

Directions

Add the oil to a small non-stick pan and heat to low. Remove the tough, dirty outer skin of the cippolini and cut both sides so that they are flat, allowing for even browning. When the oil is hot, add the onions and let brown on each side for about five minutes, or until golden. Divide one tablespoon of sugar on top of each onion, and then flip. Use the remaining tablespoon of sugar for the other side. Caramelize both sides for another five minutes each, checking for brownness frequently.

Desserts

Scalloped Apples

Ingredients

2 cups soft breadcrumbs
2 tablespoons butter
3 cups apples
½ cup sugar
¼ teaspoon cinnamon
½ teaspoon nutmeg

½ lemon, juice and rind
¼ cup water

Directions

Directions:

Butter the breadcrumbs. Chop or cut the apples in small pieces, and add the remaining ingredients to the apples. Put ¼ of the crumbs in the bottom of a buttered baking dish, add ½ of the apple mixture, then ¼ of the crumbs, the remainder of the apple mixture, and then cover with the remainder of the crumbs. Bake 40-60 minutes (until the apples are tender and the crumbs brown), on medium heat. Cover during the first 20 minutes of baking. Serve hot with sugar and cream.

Be careful when grating the lemon rind. Only the thin yellow portion should be used as flavoring.

Peach Cup

Ingredients

8 ripe peaches or apricots
2 eggs
½ cup milk
1 ½ cups flour
3 teaspoons baking powder
½ teaspoon salt
1 tablespoon butter
granulated sugar

Directions

Pare the peaches (or apricots), mash two of them, and add the well-beaten egg yolks. Add the milk, and then the dry ingredients (through a sifter). Melt the butter, then add it to the flour mixture. Beat well, then cut and fold in the well-beaten egg whites. Put a layer of the mixture in the bottom of a custard cup, add half a peach or apricot, and cover with batter. Sprinkle granulated sugar over the top, and bake on medium heat for 20 minutes. Turn from the cups and serve hot with whipped cream.

Orange Marmalade

Ingredients

1 dozen oranges
6 lemons
1 grapefruit
sugar

Directions

Weigh the fruit, slice it. To each pound of fruit, add one quart of cold water. Let the mixture stand for 24 hours. Then cook slowly for 2 hours. Weigh the cooked fruit. Add an equal weight of sugar. Cook for one hour or until it stiffens. Pour into sterilized canning jars, cover, and seal.

Fruit Slush

Ingredients

2 ⅔ cups cantaloupe or watermelon,
coarsely chopped, seeded, and peeled
1⅓ cups kiwi, coarsely chopped
3 packets Splenda®
2 tablespoons lime juice
2 cups water
ice

Directions

In a blender, puree fruit with Splenda® and lime juice until smooth.
Combine fruit mixture with water in large pitcher. If desired, pour
through a strainer to eliminate pulp. Stir well and pour into tall
glasses with ice.

Serves 4.

Grilled Grapes

▌ An unexpected treat from the grill!

Ingredients

6 medium clusters grapes, seedless
1 teaspoon olive oil
6 rosemary sprigs
6 thyme sprigs

Directions

Preheat grill to medium. Wash and thoroughly pat the grapes dry with paper towels. With a pastry brush, brush the grapes with oil. Tuck a rosemary and thyme sprig into each grape cluster.

Grill, turning frequently, for 15 to 20 minutes, or until the grapes develop grill marks and a few start to split.

Plum-Raspberry Dessert Soup

Try this great recipe for a fruity cold soup. It's perfect for summer entertaining!

Ingredients

8 medium (1 ½ pounds) plums, sliced
1 cup fresh or frozen raspberries
1 ½ cups dry red wine
3 sticks cinnamon
½ cup water
1 tablespoon cornstarch

3 tablespoons sugar
low-fat vanilla yogurt (optional)
mint sprigs, for garnish

Directions

In a large saucepan, combine the plums, raspberries, wine, and cinnamon sticks. Bring to a boil over medium-high heat. Reduce the heat and simmer for 15 minutes, or until the fruit is very soft.

In a cup, blend the water and cornstarch until smooth. Whisk into the soup; cook, stirring until the soup thickens and boils. Remove from the heat and add sugar to taste; remove the cinnamon sticks. Cool the soup.

In a blender, puree the soup until smooth. Pour into a covered container and refrigerate until well chilled. (Can be refrigerated up to 2 days.)

To serve, ladle the soup into shallow bowls. Drop a small scoop of frozen yogurt into the center of each serving, if desired. Garnish with mint sprigs.

Watermelon with Fresh Raspberry Sauce

Ingredients

⅓ cup raspberry vinegar
2 tablespoons sugar
1 cup (½ pint) raspberries
4 watermelon wedges with their
rind, chilled
mint sprigs, for garnish

Directions

In a small saucepan, combine the vinegar and sugar and bring to a boil over medium heat, stirring until the sugar dissolves. Remove from the heat and stir in the raspberries.

Place the watermelon wedges on plates and spoon the raspberry mixture over. Garnish with mint sprigs and serve.

Fresh Pear Cream Pie

Ingredients

5 egg yolks
¼ cup granulated sugar
finely grated rind and juice of 1 lemon
1 ¼ cups whipping cream
single crust 9-inch pie shell
4 pears, peeled, cored and quartered
3 egg whites
¾ cup superfine sugar

Directions

In a glass bowl, place 3 of the egg yolks and granulated sugar, lemon rind and juice.

Place the bowl over saucepan of simmering water.

Cook for 15 minutes, stirring constantly with a wooden spoon until mixture begins to thicken.

Remove bowl from pan. Cool to room temperature.

In another bowl, beat cream with remaining 2 egg yolks and fold into cooled lemon mixture.

Spread mixture over bottom of pie crust and then spread pears on top, pressing them in lightly.

In separate bowl, beat egg whites until foamy.

Add superfine sugar little by little, continuing to beat until mixture is shiny and forms stiff peaks.

Spread meringue over top of pie.

Bake in center of a preheated 250 °F oven for 1 hour.

Remove from oven and leave to cool for at least 6 hours in order for the custard base to settle and firm. (Can be refrigerated).

Rhubarb Crisp

Ingredients

1 pound rhubarb, chopped into
1-inch pieces
2 sweet red apples (such as Rome
or Gala), peeled, cored and sliced
½ cup orange juice
1 teaspoon ground cinnamon

3 tablespoons Splenda®
1 cup plain bread crumbs
2 tablespoons brown sugar
1 tablespoon olive oil

Directions

Preheat broiler.

In a large saucepan, combine rhubarb, apples, orange juice, cinnamon and 3 tablespoon Splenda®.

Cover and cook over medium heat for 5 to 10 minutes, or until the rhubarb is just tender.

Taste the mixture and add more Splenda® if desired.

Meanwhile, in a medium bowl, combine bread crumbs, olive oil and brown sugar (2 tablespoons).

Mix well to combine.

Spread mixture on a foil-lined baking sheet and broil until lightly toasted, about 3 minutes.

Spoon half of the bread crumb mixture into the bottom of a shallow serving dish.

Cover with the warm fruit mixture and top with remaining crumb mixture.

Serve warm.

When buying rhubarb, look for thin, crisp, dark pink to red stalks. Be sure to remove and discard the leaves before using since they are poisonous.

Carrot Oatmeal Cookies

These filling cookies are sweetened with honey for a healthy alternative to sugar.

Ingredients

1 cup honey
1 ½ teaspoons cinnamon
1 cup vegetable oil
1 teaspoon nutmeg
1 teaspoon vanilla extract
1 teaspoon allspice
2 eggs
2 cups old-fashioned oatmeal

2 cups whole-wheat flour
1 cup chopped nuts
2 teaspoons baking powder
2 cups raisins
1 teaspoon salt, or to taste
2 cups grated carrots

Directions

Preheat oven to 375 °F.

In a mixing bowl, beat together the honey, oil, vanilla, and eggs. In a large bowl, combine the flour, baking powder, salt, cinnamon, nutmeg, allspice, and oatmeal. Blend well. Then stir in the nuts, raisins, and carrots.

Add the liquid ingredients to the mixture and blend well. Drop by teaspoonfuls onto an oiled cookie sheet. Bake for 12-15 minutes or until the cookies are golden brown. Remove the cookies from the cookie sheet and cool them on a rack before storing.

Stuffed Melon with Lemon and Honey Dressing

(Courtesy of the Massachusetts Department of Agricultural Resources)

Ingredients

1 cantaloupe or other melon
2 cups fresh blueberries, washed
1 cup plain yogurt
1 tablespoon lemon juice
2 tablespoons honey

Directions

Cut melon in half and scrape out seeds from center. Heap fresh blueberries into hollowed out part of melon. Combine yogurt, lemon juice and honey. Serve about ¼ cup dressing over each bowl of berries.

Spiced Carrot Cake with Creamy Mascarpone Frosting

(Courtesy of John Scheepers Kitchen Garden Seeds, www.kitchengardenseeds.com)

Our Spiced Carrot Cake with Creamy Mascarpone Frosting makes dessert feel like a birthday party any day of the year. The diced crystallized ginger and nutmeg give the cake a rich, complex flavor and the mascarpone frosting is so delicious that you will want to eat it by the spoonful (but do try to save it for the cake). It will be everyone's favorite!

Ingredients

Cake:

3 eggs
2 cups sugar
2 cups grated carrots
1 ½ cups vegetable oil
1 cup crushed pineapple
1 tablespoon finely diced crystallized ginger
1 cup flaked coconut
2 ¼ cups flour
2 teaspoons cinnamon
½ teaspoon grated nutmeg
1 teaspoon baking powder
1 teaspoon salt
1 teaspoon vanilla extract
1 cup golden raisins
½ cup chopped walnuts

Creamy mascarpone frosting:

6 ounces cream cheese
6 ounces mascarpone cheese
½ cup unsalted butter
3 ¾ cups confectioner's sugar
1 teaspoon vanilla paste
1 teaspoon lemon zest

Directions

Preheat oven to 350 °F. Grease and flour two cake pans or two bread pans. Beat eggs lightly. Add sugar: beat until light and fluffy. Mix in carrots. Add oil, pineapple, crystallized ginger and coconut, mixing to blend. Add dry ingredients and vanilla: mix until just blended. By hand, stir in raisins and walnuts. Bake in prepared pans for one hour. Let sit at room temperature to cool. Remove from cake pans to cooling racks.

Beat room temperature cream cheese, mascarpone cheese and butter together. Add confectioner's sugar in parts, beating slowly to blend. Add vanilla extract and lemon zest, blending until smooth. Frost cooled cakes. For fun, garnish with long, skinny microplaned, sugar-coated carrot ribbons.

Pumpkin Crème Caramel

(Courtesy of John Scheepers Kitchen Garden Seeds, www.kitchengardenseeds.com)

> There is nothing better than savoring the goodness of homegrown vegetables and herbs through winter's cold, dark months. Like serving my own pesto bubbling atop warm goat cheese with crackers, or sneaking into the freezer for my choice of herbed butters, or serving my pumpkin crème caramel on Thanksgiving.

Ingredients

1 cup sugar
1 cup heavy cream
1 cup milk
1 tablespoon vanilla paste
3 eggs
2 egg yolks
½ cup sugar
½ cup cooked pumpkin puree
pinch of ground cloves, cinnamon
and nutmeg (optional)

Directions

Pour one cup of sugar into a heavy skillet. Slowly melt the sugar until it is a smooth, golden caramel. Pour the caramel into a 1 ½ quart soufflé dish, swirling it around to cover the bottom and 3 inches up the sides. Place the soufflé dish in a baking pan of cold water.

Combine the heavy cream, milk and vanilla paste in a saucepan. Heat to scalding and simmer for 8 minutes. In a large bowl, whip the eggs and egg yolks until frothy. Slowly add ½ cup sugar, blending well. Add the cooked pumpkin puree, beating until well incorporated and smooth. Add ever so small pinches of ground cloves, cinnamon and nutmeg if you like.

In steady stream, pour the hot cream mixture into the egg mixture while whisking. Pour the custard into the soufflé dish. Bake at 350 °F for one hour. Let it cool. Once cool, invert the crème caramel onto a larger plate with sides to catch the delicious caramel. Serve with a dollop of freshly whipped cream sweetened with brown sugar and a hint of vanilla.

To make cooked pumpkin puree, select a beautiful Rouge d'Etampes, Spooktacular or Long Island Cheese pumpkin. Each pound produces about one cup of puree. Cut the pumpkin in half and scoop out the seeds and fibers. Wipe the surface with a paper towel dipped in canola oil. Place the pumpkin halves on a baking sheet, fill with about an inch of water and cover with foil. Bake in a preheated 350 °F oven for 60 to 90 minutes or until the pumpkin flesh is soft and tender when pierced with a knife.

References

Books

Barash, Cathy Wilkinson. *Kitchen Gardens: How to Create a Beautiful and Functional Culinary Garden.* Houghton Mifflin Company 1998.

Bartholomew, Mel. *Square Foot Gardening: A New Way to Garden in Less Space with Less Work.* Rodale Press, Inc. 2005.

Cuthbertson, Yvonne. *Success with Organic Vegetables.* Guild of Master Craftsman Publications Ltd 2006.

Peel, Lucy. *Kitchen Gardens: What to Grow and How to Grow It.* Harper Collins Publishers Inc. 2003.

Websites

American Community Gardening Association
www.communitygarden.org

American Feast's Sustainable Food Blog
blog.americanfeast.com

Avant-Gardening: Creative Organic Gardening
www.avant-gardening.com

Ball® Brand Fresh Preserving
www.freshpreserving.com

Garden Guides
www.gardenguides.com

The National Gardening Association
www.garden.org/home

The Old Farmer's Almanac
www.almanac.com

Pick Your Own
www.pickyourown.org

Vegetable Garden Planning
vegetablegardenplanning.net

The Vegetable Patch
www.thevegetablepatch.com

My Recipes

My Recipes

My Recipes

My Recipes

My Recipes

My Recipes

My Recipes

My Recipes

My Recipes

My Recipes

My Recipes